HELEN MORGAN
Her Life and Legend

Other Books by GILBERT MAXWELL

POETRY
  Look to the Lightning
  Stranger's Garment
  The Dark Rain Falling
  Go Looking (Selected Poems)
FICTION
  The Sleeping Trees
BIOGRAPHY
  Tennessee Williams and Friends

HELEN MORGAN
Her Life and Legend

Gilbert Maxwell

HAWTHORN BOOKS, INC.
Publishers/NEW YORK

Quotation on pages 94–95 from review by Howard Thompson of October 2, 1967, © 1967 by The New York Times Company. Reprinted by permission.

Poem on page 184 by Hilaire Belloc from *Sonnets and Verse*, Duckworth and Company, London. Reprinted by permission.

Library of Congress Catalog Card Number: 73-21319
ISBN: 0-8015-4526-9

1 2 3 4 5 6 7 8 9 10

To
Helga Eason

Contents

Acknowledgments

First of all, my thanks are due to George Blackwood, whose vivid memories of Miss Morgan have obviously served as the backbone of this book. Secondly, my heartfelt gratitude to Michael Angelano, head of Art and Music at the Miami Public Library, Main Branch, for his tireless, efficient cooperation in research.

I am also indebted to Donald Prince and Sara Sanders Thomas, of Atlanta; to Richard Orme, a member of the *Show Boat* revival company; and to Claire Luce for recollections of Miss Morgan during the 1930s.

HELEN MORGAN
Her Life and Legend

1

Helen and Jerry and "Bill"

IF THE SAGA OF HELEN MORGAN, Jerome Kern, and their "Bill" should ever fall into the hands of a hack TV scriptwriter, he'd almost certainly reach into his memory's ragbag for old-time radio's favorite title, "A Date with Destiny."

Like most ten-twenty-thirty melodramas of the florid nineties, the factual plot of the piece would strain the credulity of any boob-box addict with an I.Q. of eighty-seven. The tale has a mawkish middle as well as a monstrous end, and any one of several brashly coincidental beginnings could serve as an opening scene.

Perhaps, though, it all began for Helen Morgan at a summer evening performance of *Americana*, a minor Broadway revue in which she was not listed in the program among the principals.

On this particular evening the house lights dimmed and a white spot picked out, in the orchestra pit, a wistful waif perched on top of an upright piano. The waif raised her tousled head, half closed her luminous hazel eyes, and trilled the first notes of Philip Charig's blues ballad, "Nobody Wants Me."

Morgan sang the song in her seemingly small voice that actually could range from plaintive high to throaty low, and each true note, each lilting, limpid word winged out to hold her listeners enthralled.

On this night, as on all others, Helen's audience sat transfixed by that sweet voice, rising, falling, clear as crystal water, surging up from a wellspring of totally honest emotion. And no listener was more attentive than a small, bespectacled man down front who looked, in his black and white tuxedo, like nothing so much as a droll, sleek-coated penguin.

The small man's name was Kern, and whether he had been told to go and hear this singer at the Belmont Theater, or whether he'd come because some of *Americana*'s songs were the work of his good friends George and Ira Gershwin, is not a matter of record, and no matter. The important point of our cliché, chance discovery plot is this: that Jerry Kern had appeared just at this time in a struggling, unknown artist's life to cast, as penguins do, the shiny pebble of courtship at the feet of Helen Morgan, in order that he might mate her with his "Bill."

Kern had been slaving for months with Oscar Hammerstein II on the score of a revolutionary musical play adapted from Edna Ferber's best-selling novel *Show Boat*. Most of the parts had been cast, but he was still in search of a subtly different, honestly emotional singer who could also act—a special someone, not merely to play but to *become* the tragic mixed-blood heroine Julie Dozier, identified in Ferber's book as "the best damned actress" on any show boat plying the Mississippi.

Until this night Kern had been gravely concerned as to how and where a consummate Julie could be found. Now, as he sat absorbing Helen Morgan's poignant cry against going on living in a lonesome world where nobody wanted her, his mind rapped out, staccato: "Here she is. Right *here*. Here's my Julie."

Suddenly, as the last deep-throated note drifted away, Morgan lowered her head and a moment of silence held the packed house suspended in willing disbelief. Then a typhoon of applause swelled up from the orchestra, past the mezzanine and the balconies, to reach the Belmont's rafters. Tonight— as on all other nights since this revue had opened—a former biscuit packer, sales clerk, practical nurse, lingerie model, beauty contest winner from Toronto, Canada, by way of Danville, Illinois, had, in making her magic, stopped *Americana* cold.

Jerry Kern stayed on through the show. He may or may not have gone back afterward to tell Morgan what he had in mind for her, but one thing has been recorded. He left the Belmont knowing he'd found a Julie who could handle a highly special song that had been waiting, like a humbly patient lover, nine long years for her.

Now the *Show Boat* score would read, with a single exception, "Music and Lyrics by Jerome Kern and Oscar Hammerstein II." The exception would of course be "Bill"—music by Jerome Kern, lyrics by P. G. Wodehouse. And here again, in the alliance of Helen and "Bill," the lengthy arm of coincidence, plus two incidents involving improbable cause and effect, came into play.

This was the summer of 1927, and Kern and Wodehouse had written "Bill" in 1918 for their Princess Theater musical *Oh, Lady, Lady,* but the song had turned out to be "unsuitable" for the star, Vivienne Segal. So "Bill" was put back into Kern's portfolio to stay until 1920, when his composers tried to ally him with Marilyn Miller in Florenz Ziegfeld's *Sally.* Once again, however, because the delectable blonde star's voice was too light to range high and low over this poetic ballad of an *ordinary man,* "Bill" was dropped from the score of the Ziegfeld production; and because Miss Miller was then the brightest musical-comedy luminary, nobody dreamed of teaming "Bill" with an obscure dark-haired singer named Helen Morgan, moodily prancing about in *Sally*'s chorus.

Now on this summer night as Jerry Kern walked away from the Belmont, his head was filled with plans for "Bill" and the girl from the rear row of *Sally.* Until this night he'd intended to have every song in *Show Boat* express the character or situation for which it had been created. Now he'd decided to make a place for "Bill" in the score, and even as Helen Morgan sat in a communal dressing room removing her makeup in the midst of other chattering minor players, the wheel of fortune—as they say in the sudsy serials—had begun to spin for her. She would soon be keeping her date with "Bill" (and with Destiny) at the New Amsterdam Theater in a Ziegfeld super-production.

Show Boat, with music and lyrics except for one song by Kern and Hammerstein, was about to achieve a major breakthrough in the history of American musicals. And because of that one exceptional song, the lifelong partnership of Helen and "Bill" would be contracted. A new star was in the making, but her name would not go up in lights above the title of *Show Boat* until the fall of 1932, five years after that name had winked from the roofs of three old New York mansions that housed a trio of fabulous, federal-raided nightclubs called, in succession, Helen Morgan's 54th Street Club, Chez Morgan, and Helen Morgan's Summer Home.

Helen was named after her mother's mother, and, reader, "that's all there is, there isn't any more" to be learned about the lady's grandparents on either side of the house, nor for that matter, about her father's origin, nor the years of his life before he became a fireman on the Canadian National Railroad.

Research reveals just this: one year, or maybe a year and a half, before the turn of the century, Thomas Morgan, a handsome, swashbuckling Irishman who looked considerably like the screen idol Francis X. Bushman, met and courted a comely farm girl from upstate New York whose given name was Lulu.

Where and when the couple first got acquainted remains a mystery, but it would seem likely the scene was Saratoga Springs since Lulu and Tom were both lifelong devotees of the sport of kings—and because the farm that was Lulu's birthplace bordered on the St. Lawrence River in a district near the Saratoga tracks where, on a clear day in the declining nineties, the hoi polloi could gaze upon the legendary Lillian Russell and her constant, attentive escort, the corpulent, jovial Diamond Jim Brady.

So much for likely conjecture. Suffice it to say that somewhere, somehow, Lulu and Tom got married, and (this is for sure) lived together for a short time in a small house near the railroad tracks in Toronto, Canada.

One day in the winter of 1900, when Tom learned that his wife was pregnant, he lit out for parts undesignated, leaving his spouse—in the best tradition of show boat melodrama—to deal singlehanded with a situation for which he was surely 50 percent responsible.

But if Tom ran true to form as a stage villain, Lulu side-stepped the role of the frightened, deserted stage heroine who invariably headed back to the old homestead. Instead, she decided to stick it out in Toronto, perhaps because her parents had warned her that if she made her bed with a bibulous Irish racetrack tout she'd have to lie in it alone, or because the dubious existence of a grass widow, *enceinte*, sheltered, fed, yet subjected to a sweetly forbearing silence or the constant, maddening reminder, "I told you so," held small appeal for an independent spirit.

The latter conjecture seems logical, for this young country woman bore no resemblance, in pride and intestinal stamina, to the wronged females of her day as they were portrayed on the boards, or between the covers of such pious paperback novels as *Beulah* and *Bertha, the Sewing Machine Girl*.

Lulu never talked too much about herself, but it is a fact that, on the day Tom Morgan took a walk, she put on her hat and coat, marched herself down to the roundhouse lunchroom in Toronto's railroad yard, and asked for a job.

Looking straight at the owner out of her great gray-blue eyes that made men forget the set of the jaw in her angular face, Lulu stated her qualifications. As a country girl, she'd been used to serving up victuals in a hurry to hungry farmhands. Also, she could roll up her sleeves and help with the dishes at a rush time, or even—if push came to shove—lend a capable hand at the range.

The lunchroom's owner listened and nodded. It so happened he did need another girl on the early day shift from six in the morning until two in the afternoon, so he told her to come to work next day.

Lulu was attractive, efficient, and blessed with a sharp sense of humor, so she got on fine with the boss and the tough railroad men. Still, her wages were nominal and a dime was a fair-sized tip in the year 1900. She could barely keep up the rent on her house, so Lulu worked, slow on her feet, right up to and including the day when her labor pains began.

This doughty woman never went into detail as to how she managed, that autumn night, to have her baby, alone in the house with neither doctor nor midwife. She would only tell, with a kind of crook-mouthed pride, how she rose and went back to work the next morning, carrying her infant, wrapped warm in a market basket under her arm.

It was October in Canada and the day was already cold, so she placed the basket behind the stove in the lunchroom, and the space between the iron range and the wall began to serve as Helen Morgan's daytime nursery.

This being the case, it was natural that the greasy spoon's boss and the railroad stiffs should begin to feel a proprietary interest in the bundle behind the stove. Long before she could toddle, Helen was bounced on the knees of the men to the measures of haunting French Canadian folk songs, as well as rocked to sleep with the racetrack ditties that Lulu crooned to her, in lieu of conventional lullabies.

All her life Morgan remembered these songs, and when the mood was on her she could be heard in her dressing room softly humming, "Camptown ladies sing this song, doo da, doo da," or singing in authentic Canadian French some pensive rural ballad of heartbreak and lifelong loss.

When his daughter was four years old, Tom Morgan suddenly returned to knock on the door of the small house near the railroad yards, and his lonely wife, relenting, let him in.

Tom now had a job on the Pennsylvania Railroad, and he wanted to make a home for his family, so Lulu said good-by to the gang at the lunchroom, packed up, and set off, with her self-styled reformed better half, for Illinois.

Things were easier for Lulu in the manufacturing town of Danville. She had more time to spend with her little girl, and she always loved to recall a Saturday morning when Helen, just turned five, climbed up on her ironing board and announced, as though to an audience, "I will now sing 'Three Blind Mice.' "

Lulu set the iron aside and listened; then, as the last note quavered out, she cried, "Marvelous, my darling. Some day you'll be a great big star and make a million dollars. What will you do with it all?"

Her daughter proffered a kiss. "Spend it and give it away," she said—and time and again, as the grown-up Helen's salary rocketed, and her reckless generosity exceeded all reason, Lulu would shake her head in dismay, recalling that distant morning. It was as if this willful daughter of hers had actually known from the start that once she'd begun to make big money she'd not only be spending it on countless luxuries for Lulu and herself but giving it away unhesitatingly to any casual acquaintance, deserving or no, who came to her for a loan.

If ever an individual could have been called generous to a fault, it was Helen Morgan, and no remonstrance from Lulu or anyone else would ever stay her profligate hand. She had always been a giver, not a taker, and the instinct for giving, if inborn, was certainly strengthened by the deprivations of a poverty-ridden early adolescence, for Tom Morgan, despite all his grand talk about reformation, had not come home, when she was four years old, to play the role of a permanent loving provider.

At some time between 1905 and 1912 (the year when a Big Thing happened to Helen) this restless, gambling railroad man once again climbed down from his caboose at the end of a day's run to head out for distant places, and Lulu was left again to make out as best she could in a house beside the tracks.

In those days Danville, Illinois, was the trade center of a farming and dairying area where factories turned out textiles, hardware, paper boxes, mining machinery, bricks, and candy, so Lulu Morgan may for a time have boxed candy or assembled paper boxes—but certainly not after the summer of 1912 when a writer from the Chicago *Daily News* visited Danville's railroad yards to gather data for a feature story on the wives of railroad men.

The writer was Amy Leslie, a former actress with the stage

name of Lillie West. At this time Miss Leslie was fifty-one years old, and she always showed up at Chicago first nights, a familiar spectacle in bright-colored shawls, scarves, and furs, wielding an elegant staff as she made her way down the aisle to her house seat.

Amy was one of the Toddlin' Town's true characters, so it is not surprising that this short-statured, plump woman with frizzed-up, dyed red hair, stopped dead while casing the Pennsylvania Railroad's roundhouse, intrigued by another character who was pursuing a pleasurable daily occupation.

What Miss Leslie saw and heard that afternoon was the preteenaged Miss Morgan, perched on the cowcatcher of an engine on the roundhouse turnstile, entertaining the railroad stiffs with a French Canadian ballad.

La Morgan was singing in a surprisingly mature voice, unaware of fate in the person of this painted lady with flaming hair, but by the time she'd finished her number the die was cast. And even as she slipped off the cowcatcher, embarrassed by the lady's appreciative cries and applause, her carefree days in the old roundhouse with her railroad buddies were numbered.

Amy Leslie went home with the girl to meet Lulu, who was certainly in a position to give any writer a résumé of the life of a railroad man's wife (or widow). By this time, however, Amy was more interested in taking on, as a lifetime protégée, the waif whose act she'd caught in the roundhouse.

She told Lulu Morgan that her daughter had great talent and instinctive showmanship. She may also have said that she —Miss Leslie, formerly Lillie West—was in a position to know, though she undoubtedly did not give herself the kind of full treatment she later received in Sophie Tucker's autobiography, *Some of These Days*. Miss Leslie was, said Sophie, by reason of "her penetrating mind . . . her fearless and witty pen," a figure of power in show business, respected by managers, producers, stars, and lesser troupers.

Performers whose careers she had helped to establish had filled her suite at the Parkway Hotel with gifts of "rare and beautiful things," including a fabulous array of clocks and a collection of oversized, costly handbags, constantly replenished by such big-time producer friends as Ziegfeld, Belasco, the Frohman brothers, Al Woods, C. B. Dillingham, and Sam Harris.

Miss Amy Leslie was a force to be reckoned with in the world of the theater, and as she talked with Helen's mother she outlined a plan for her new protégée. Having been on the staff of a Montreal newspaper, she had a good friend in Jack Mercereau of the prominent Mercereau family, which owned a couple of nightclubs in the French quarter of that city. She would contact Jack about giving Helen a tryout at his Club Gabiorenden, or his smaller basement club, the French Trocadero.

She said good-by, promising to get in touch with Lulu as soon as she had something definite to offer Helen.

Days passed like so many years for Lulu and Helen; then a letter came saying that Amy had been able to arrange for a tryout engagement at thc French Troc. She mentioned a near date for the Morgans' departure for Montreal, and assured them that she would meet their train at the station.

Lulu packed with a will, as she had done in Toronto, and neither she nor her eager daughter felt the slightest regret at leaving behind a life of penury near the tracks of Danville, Illinois. Helen had abandoned the roundhouse turnstile on a spin of fortune's wheel. And if she was even half as good as Miss Amy Leslie claimed, she ought to make out as well as the next one, in Montreal.

Now, according to the rules of routine theatrical biography, this is the point where the youthful aspirant to fame and fortune should fail her audition and leave the French Troc, suicidal, with the words of a gruff but kindly cigar-chewing manager echoing in her ears to the tune of something like this: "Tough luck, kid. You may have the stuff but you're just too young, see? Come back in a coupla years when you're able to fill out a bra."

Nothing of the sort, as a matter of actual fact, occurred. Helen Morgan, twelve years old, pleased both the pianist and

the French Troc's manager at her tryout, and went over on
her opening night with a bang that reverberated by word of
mouth from that night's sparse audience throughout the
Canadian city. She sang the traditional French Canadian folk
songs, twanged the strings of the customers' hearts with "Old
Virginny," and held even the barflies spellbound.

Prior to this memorable evening, the barman in the little
basement spot had been lucky to serve a dozen customers a
night. One week later the place was so packed that only an
inner circle of patrons could see or hear the wistful warbler,
and (contrary to a couple of other stories) this was the first
time Helen Morgan was picked up and placed, by an
unknown, enterprising admirer, on top of an upright piano.
This is the way Helen always told it, and it is actually how,
as a half-grown songbird, she made a figurative overnight leap
from a railroad engine's cowcatcher to the top of a battered
upright in a Montreal cellar saloon.

Her success in the little club was remarkable, but she was
soon forced to abandon her perch and return to school, after
a visit to the Troc by a bluenose from the vigilant Gerry Society, whose meddling members frowned upon what they considered child exploitation in every phase of show business.

Helen and Lulu returned to live on Chicago's West Side,
and the fall of 1913 found Helen attending Crane High School
and Sunday School at a Congregational church.

Just how Lulu managed financially at this time is not
entirely clear, but she must have been able to save something
out of Helen's Troc salary. Also, it is possible to conjecture
that the big-hearted Amy Leslie, who'd be keeping this protégée under her wing for years, slipped her mother something
out of her own sizable salary.

As for Helen, just entering her teens in the fall of 1913,
she seems to have left Crane High School as a freshman, to
pack crackers for the National Biscuit Company at a salary of
eight dollars a week. She moved from there to a job at nine
dollars a week, pouring scoops of gelatine powder into waxed
paper bags that she stuffed in boxes, until she got fired for
consuming the profits.

She remembered ruefully, "Somehow I took a liking to the damned stuff. They caught me eating it and canned me."

She went on to another job at six dollars a week, sticking prizes in boxes at a Cracker Jack plant, but there too (because of her compulsive generosity) she received a dismissal slip. It seemed she could seldom resist slipping two prizes into a Cracker Jack box, because she "was always thinking about the surprise some kid would get."

After that she tried dunning the Chicago Telephone Company's recalcitrant customers for overdue bills, but the project made her so sad she had to quit.

In later years when Morgan, the star, reminisced about this rugged time in her life, she never explained that she couldn't help wanting to make some kid happy with two Cracker Jack prizes because her own childhood had been blighted, nor did she say that she ate the gelatine powder out of necessity, but once, after she'd become a celebrity, when someone asked the reason for her success, she answered, "Hunger."

While other girls who were well fed and well dressed danced and dated their way through Crane High School, Helen served time as a practical nurse, clerked behind a ribbon counter at Marshall Fields, and finally became a manicurist. She took "elocution" from her Congregational Sunday school teacher, whose brother was a booking agent, and when she was just eighteen that enterprising young man got her an audition at a place called the Green Mill, where she made her first professional appearance in Chicago.

She might have stayed at the Mill for a while if she hadn't entered and won a statewide beauty contest. She was crowned Miss Illinois, and then some friends, including Amy Leslie, made up a pot to send her to Canada, where she entered a second tourney from which she emerged as Miss Mount Royal.

When she returned to Chicago, she characteristically parceled out a considerable part of her fifteen hundred dollars in prize money to friends who had backed her. But this was not to be the end, for now her imaginative young press agent friend dispatched her to New York, where, surely by previous arrangement, he'd contrived to have his client met by a former engineer for the Brooklyn Rapid Transit Company known as Red Mike, who had become New York's controversial mayor, John F. Hylan.

This red-headed, red-moustached mick had been fired from the BRT by a superintendent who swore that Red Mike Hylan, at the throttle of a subway engine, had chased him while he was casing the tracks prior to appearing as a witness at a coroner's inquest regarding a collision in which a fireman friend of Hylan's had been killed.

After being fired, Hylan studied law at night and became, in due time, a Brooklyn judge whose hatred ranged from subway superintendents to all BRT financial bigwigs. Later, when he became mayor of New York, his campaigns to maintain a nickel subway fare relieved the financiers' coffers of more than a million dollars in profits.

Hylan was a heavy-built, stodgy, innately suspicious man with few social graces, who alienated the metropolitan press by referring to newspaper men as "conniving scavengers." However, as Helen's agent may have discovered, he was an irreproachable husband and father who could be appealed to on behalf of a railroad fireman's daughter, and the day of Helen's arrival at Penn Station marked one of just two occasions when Hylan was in rare good humor with the public and the press.

The first was on the day of the false armistice in 1918. At that time, surrounded by a police guard and about to be photographed outside City Hall, Hylan ordered two of New York's Finest to release a belligerent drunk and allow him to speak his mind, only to be confounded by the following excoriation: "Red Mike, I knew you when you was fired as an engineer from the BRT. You was a son of a bitch then, Red Mike, and you're a son of a bitch now."

The mayor fared better, though, at Pennsylvania Station on the afternoon when he and the men from the Manhattan dailies assembled there to greet Miss Mount Royal.

As Helen stepped down from the Pullman car, His Honor sprang forward to clasp her hand and acclaim her as "a Canadian beauty."

This was a truly joyous occasion, and Helen must have entered the official limousine in a high-hearted mood. She had come to the big town bringing, in her suitcase, the gold-lettered, blue satin ribbon with which she'd paraded triumphantly before the Canadian judges. And now here she was, riding beside the mayor of New York, with a story about to break in the next day's papers—so how could she fail to gain immediate access to the inner offices of the most important theatrical producers, including the great Flo Ziegfeld himself?

The girl must have looked out, wildly excited, at the drab daylight spectacle of Broadway, but if she'd even so much as suspected how long it would take her to get her trim foot inside the door of a trustworthy theatrical agent's office—much less on the mat outside a producer's sanctum—she might well have decided to catch the night train back to Chicago.

Throughout the first few weeks of her new life in New York, this "different"-looking Irish girl with the milk-white, heart-shaped face, the heavy-lashed hazel eyes looking out from under a mop of darkly shining hair, subsisted, like many another stage-struck youngster, on waning enthusiasm, false promises, and constant hope. Helen may, in fact, have fared worse than her sisters who succumbed to the current vogue of ratted ear puffs, layers of paint, and purple lipstick, precisely because she did cling to her gamine coiffure and refrained from rouging, plucking her eyebrows, or beading her lashes with lampblack. In short, Miss Helen Morgan looked like nobody except her naturally beautiful self, and this may have caused her to seem, to unimaginative agents and musical show producers, like a maverick in a herd of branded fillies.

When Lulu came on to New York, the two women shared a double room in the apartment of Anne Wheaton, an actress friend of Helen's, at West Seventy-second Street and the Hudson River.

In 1918, with the war fever at a peak, Helen, who could get no work in the theater, did the next best thing patriotically, not to say publicity-wise.

One afternoon, ending the footsore rounds of the casting offices, she and Lulu paused in the tiny park opposite the Palace Theater (now known as Father Duffy Square) to hear Miss Gracie Fields belt out war songs from the back of an army truck.

On the truck assisting Miss Fields was Edith Day, the star of *Irene*—and the small blonde sprite with golden curls seated at a table selling Liberty bonds was none other than Gladys Smith, known to the world at large as Mary Pickford, America's sweetheart.

Miss Morgan and her mother conferred briefly in an undertone; then, as Gracie stepped back to rest her voice, the two approached the bond table.

Helen took a big breath and asked, "Miss Pickford, if we buy a ten-dollar bond, would Miss Fields let me sing a song?"

Miss Pickford smiled as she asked, "What would you like to sing, dear?" And Lulu answered, "My daughter knows the words to 'Over There.' "

They bought the bond, and Gracie, who needed no mouthpiece to be heard down at Times Square, passed the megaphone to Helen Morgan.

Helen sang "Over There" clearly and sweetly, and that's how the crowd around the truck heard the small, perfect voice of Helen Morgan in the open air on Broadway, just across from the Palace where, nine years later, her name would flash in lights from the big marquee.

But things were really tough for the Morgans now, so Lulu arranged with Anne Wheaton to clean the flat and make beds, thus reducing the Morgans' rent from $12.50 to $6.00 a week.

This set-up continued until Lawrence Wheaton, their hostess's actor husband, going on the road with his Broadway dramatic success, *Experience*, decided to take his wife along in a minor role.

Regretfully, Miss Wheaton gave up the apartment, and the Morgans moved into a room in a flat at 6 West 77th Street with a landlady named Eleanor Millington.

Now the ox was truly in the ditch, so Lulu went to work as

a saleswoman at Gimbels. Helen could not quite give up hope, so she persisted in trudging down to the casting offices, but she also offered her services to the Art Students League (anything except nudes). This piece work led to posing for "step in" ads, and finally to the Carnegie Hall studio of Charles Dana Gibson and Harrison Fisher's studio in the Hotel des Artistes.

At Gibson's studio Helen and another young thespian, who also posed for the artist, somehow never ran into each other.

This young man's name was George Blackwood. He was just getting a start in the New York theater, and it was not surprising that Gibson had chosen him as a dark-haired, hazel-eyed foil for his beautiful Gibson girls, since this six-foot-two, lanky Ohioan would one day be chosen, in an international contest, one of the ten most handsome men in the world.

In the year 1919 he was eighteen years old and Helen Morgan was nineteen. Exactly thirteen years later, these two would meet at the St. Regis Hotel under circumstances that would be advantageous to both. But for now the beautiful pair were entering and leaving the Carnegie Hall studios at different times, unaware of each other's existence yet mutually preoccupied with an identical problem: how to survive in New York until that elusive but surely inevitable day when one big break would open the door to stardom.

Inasmuch as Helen was not in the theater, she naturally took no part in the history-making actors' strike in the summer and fall of 1919, but she did spend a number of evenings at the Actors' Canteen, dancing with lonesome doughboys about whom she once said, marveling, "I don't see how some of 'em ever got by on the drill field. Most of the ones I danced with had two left feet."

2

The Burgeoning
Broadway Personality

AT THE START OF 1920 Helen was still looking for a spot in a show or supper club, so on January 16 she probably paid no particular attention to an event of ominous national importance that would eventually cause her almost unbearable humiliation and anguish.

It was at midnight on this date that the Eighteenth Amendment formally went into effect, paving the way for gang wars, wholesale murder, and a nightmare season of constant harassment later on, in 1928, that would drive Helen Morgan, then New York's most fabulous nightclub hostess-*chanteuse*, to the brink of nervous prostration.

Meanwhile, the winter and spring of 1920 dragged uneventfully by for her. Then in the summer she received a call from an agent who had arranged an audition for Ziegfeld's production of *Sally*, which was to star Marilyn Miller, the dancing golden sprite already established as the crown princess of American musical comedy.

Helen went to the New Amsterdam Theater expecting to sing, but before she could get her arrangements out of her briefcase the unpredictable Mr. Ziegfeld walked down front, looked her up and down, nodded, and told her, "You've got good teeth, Miss Morgan. Now walk to the wall and back."

Puzzled but eager to please, Miss Morgan did as she was

told—then suddenly heard herself being briskly assigned to the chorus by a businesslike stage manager.

She cried out, "No, Mr. Ziegfeld, please. I'm a singer, not a dancer." But the great man had already turned his attention to other matters, so she took her place in the line, crying loud enough, she hoped, to catch the boss's attention, "You watch, I'll make my mark singing or die in the attempt."

She could have saved her breath, for Florenz Ziegfeld, the impresario, was now completely absorbed in appraising the long-legged showgirls he'd contracted to glorify.

Sally was a lavish musical with songs by Guy Bolton, B. G. De Sylva, Jerome Kern, and Clifford Grey, costumes and settings by Ziegfeld's brilliant perennial artist, Joseph Urban —all tailored as much as possible for its enchanting heroine. Marilyn Miller received a salary of three thousand dollars a week, and Mr. Ziegfeld, for the first time with any star in his employ, gave her a generous percentage of the show's box office take.

On opening night, December 21, six times as many patrons as the New Amsterdam could hold were turned away, and Alexander Woollcott closed his review by saying that he had left the theater thinking first not of the song composers, Joseph Urban, the leading male comedian Leon Errol, nor even of Marilyn Miller, but of Mr. Ziegfeld because he was "that kind of producer." Said Woollcott, "There are not many of them in the world."

He noted that Miss Miller had "gone searching about and returned with a voice . . . singing now as never before," and by this back-handed compliment seemed to imply that before this season Marilyn hadn't been equipped with much of a voice —an actual fact that made it all the more ironical that a beautiful railroad fireman's daughter with a voice that could charm the birds from the boughs in Central Park was doggedly kicking about in *Sally*'s chorus, too far back to be noticed.

Morgan's name in the program was listed in such fine print that the average first-nighter couldn't have noticed it, either, and nobody in the audience—least of all Mr. Ziegfeld—even remembered that she was in the show at all. Nevertheless, though Helen herself had no possible reason to suspect it, this inauspicious job represented a kind of stalemate breakthrough for her on Broadway—and, strangely enough, the beginning of the end for Marilyn Miller as the Big Street's greatest attraction, since *Sally* was destined to be her last outstanding hit.

For Helen Morgan this show's long run meant only a means of paying the rent, buying groceries, and putting aside a little something in case of a lean season. Still, she was on her way, and when *Sally* closed after 570 performances in February 1922 she received an almost immediate offer to work in cabaret at Chicago's Cafe Montmartre.

She stayed there for several weeks, then returned to New York and signed a contract to sing for Billy Rose's hoodlum and haute monde clientele in his first modest nightspot, the Backstage Club, above a West Fifty-sixth Street garage.

It was here, according to Rose, that Morgan was first hoisted onto the top of an upright piano, after he'd been forced to set out so many tables on opening night that she had no floor space in which to work.[1] Another story had it that the sports and short-story writer Ring Lardner bounced her up there, saying he was "always interested in helping young people up to fame," and *Time* ran a picture of him and Helen to prove it.

Rose makes no mention of this in his autobiography, but he does speak of a singular visitor who dropped in on him shortly after the club's opening, and it may have been on this occasion that Helen, in rehearsal, first laid eyes on an authentic hood, in a gray fedora, conversing with her pint-sized employer.[2]

Prior to this character's initial call, Billy, in two police raids, had barely been able to smash the few bottles of booze he kept on ice in the kitchen sink before the cops got past his

---

[1] The reader, by now, knows better.
[2] Billy Rose, *Wine, Women and Words* (New York: Simon and Shuster, 1946, 1947, 1948), p. 84.

"iron door." Then, on the day following raid number two, the guy in the gray fedora turned up, placed a roll of C-notes on a table, and told the Backstage Club's harassed proprietor, "I think you can use a partner. I'd like to buy twenty-five percent of the joint!"

Billy asked, "Who said anything about needing a partner?"

The gent picked up his greenbacks, sighing, "Think it over. I'll be back tomorrow." Then, as the fedora vanished through the door, Rose asked a waiter, "Who's that guy?" and the man answered, "Arnold Rothstein's bodyguard. Everybody likes him, especially the cops. If he were your partner, you wouldn't have to smash your liquor every night."

That night the cops came for the third time, so, when the Rothstein bodyguard dropped by next day, Billy made a deal with him, accepted a roll of bills, and began a peaceful period of operation, free of police intrusion.

The Backstage Club stayed open half a year, and Helen and Rose grew accustomed to some hit man's tossing a single grand-note on a table to supply champagne for the house until all the small bills the grand had been broken into found their way into the till.

Rose had nothing but contempt for these hoods, who had no way of making themselves welcome in any place except a nightclub, where, by throwing their bloodstained loot around, they could play at being bigshots. Furthermore, it was Billy's opinion, as a man involved in Manhattan Island's night world, that "Broadway during Prohibition was as glamorous as a thumb in the eye."

It was different with Helen Morgan. Reticent and tactful by nature, she never had much to say about the ghouls from gangland who showed up at the Backstage Club, nor even about any of the big-time mobsters she came to know casually over the years.

This was because, after she'd become identified with the clubs that bore her name, she numbered among her fans several gentlemanly types from the underworld who offered her the homage and protection they felt was due a gentle lady *chanteuse* who, in the lingo of Damon Runyon, was revered by one and all in the group that gathered to munch cheesecake at Mindy's.

On the other hand, Helen took a dim view of the diminutive Mr. Rose, who gradually came to be known, after his Hippodrome production, *Jumbo*, as the "Bantam Barnum." She frequently referred to him as "the smelly Mr. Rose" because of "his heavy perfume," and once, when someone asked her why the reporters sometimes referred to Billy as "the Little Napoleon," she cried, "Why, don't you know, dear? Because he's always got his right hand inside his shirt front, feeling his left teat."

This droll observation seems mild compared to Tallulah Bankhead's reference to Rose as "animated slime," but then, as anyone who ever knew Helen will testify, she could never harbor sustained hatred toward anyone, no matter how smallminded, mean, or contemptible a person might be.

She left the Backstage Club with relief on the night it closed, but nobody ever heard her complain of being mistreated by its proprietor, nor is it likely she ever actually was.

Helen was always easy to get along with, and besides, Rose was a shrewd little showman who appreciated the kind of glamor and talent this woman possessed in abundance.

After the Backstage Club closed in 1922, Morgan was out of show business until she began rehearsing for George White's *Scandals*—and it is precisely here that a conscientious biographer comes up against a hodgepodge of misinformation offered as gospel by careless theater historians.

For example, one source states blithely: "It was here [Scandals of 1925] that Helen Morgan made her entry into the Broadway Theater. She went unnoticed, was dropped, and in another two months was found in *Americana*."[3]

Nothing of the sort occurred. In order to have been "dropped" from the *Scandals* and "found" in *Americana* within "two months or so," Helen would have had to drudge "unnoticed" in the *Scandals* of 1926—an edition in which

[3] David Ewen, *New Complete Book of the American Music Theater* (New York: Holt, Rinehart and Winston, 1958, 1959, 1970), p. 176.

she didn't appear at all, since *Americana* was not staged until 1926. But this canard is as nothing compared to Marjorie Farnsworth's account in *The Ziegfeld Follies: A History in Text and Pictures*.[4]

According to Marjorie, George White once heard her at the Backstage Club, gave her a bit part in the *Scandals*, and perched her on a piano with a hidden microphone that amplified her voice. Then, as understudy to the female lead Helen Hudson, who traditionally took sick on opening night, "the magical Morgan" took over and sang her way to stardom.

Again, nothing could have been farther from the truth and here, finally, are the real facts, gleaned from the *New York Times* review of the *Scandals* edition that opened on June 22, 1925:

> PRINCIPALS, Tom Patricola, Helen Hudson, Miller and Lyles, Mr. and Mrs. Norman Phillips, Harry Fox, Dooley and Morton, Norman Phillips, Jr., Helen Wehrle, McCarthy Sisters, Alice Weaver, Albertina Rasch Ballet, Arthur Ball, Helen Morgan and others.

Instead of sickening on opening night, Helen Hudson appeared to "excellent advantage." There is no evidence that Morgan was understudying her, and far from "opening the show to wild applause," she was the only principal who wasn't mentioned by the *Times'* anonymous critic.

What, then, was the true situation regarding Morgan and George White's *Scandals*? In a tattered *Show Boat* road tour program, made up for the Cass Theater in Detroit for the night of January 1, 1933, we find these statements that come straight from the filly's mouth:

> HELEN MORGAN, the star of the Ziegfeld Show Boat, is a native of Toronto, Canada.[5]

[4] Marjorie Farnsworth, *The Ziegfeld Follies: A History in Text and Pictures* (New York: G. P. Putnam's Sons, 1956), pp. 121–22.

[5] *Who's Who in the Theater*, and all the obituaries, erroneously state that she was born in Danville, Illinois.

> Miss Amy Leslie, the noted dramatic critic of the Chicago
> *Daily News,* saw great possibilities in Miss Morgan's work
> and induced George White to engage her for the *Scandals.*
> She remained with the White organization for two seasons
> after which Florenz Ziegfeld signed the singer. She continued
> under the Ziegfeld banner until the death of the famed
> beauty glorifier.

These two poorly written paragraphs told it like it was.
George White hadn't just "heard" Helen Morgan at the Backstage Club. Once again, as guardian angel, Amy Leslie had
induced George White to give her struggling protégée a minor
break.

Plainly, since research reveals that Morgan was not in the
Scandals of 1926, the two seasons referred to in the Cass Theater program are 1924–1925.

Nothing of consequence came of those seasons, nor was
Helen "signed" by Ziegfeld immediately after she left the
Scandals in the fall of 1925. As we already know, Jerome
Kern "found" her in *Americana* and brought her to Flo Zieg-
feld's attention. Why, then, didn't Helen see to it that the road
tour *Show Boat* program gave credit to Jerry Kern as well as
Amy Leslie?

The answer (after a careful study of Miss Morgan's brilliant, all-too-brief career) is tragically obvious. In the autumn
of 1932, distressed and sad for reasons later to be revealed
here, this woman had begun to drift day and night through a
haze of Hennessy's Three-Star brandy.

Before the autumn of 1933 the exhausted star of a super-
production that had been reduced on the road to a truncated
vaudeville revue would rally her forces for a triumphant
engagement at a swank Manhattan club. But in the first month
of that trying year she was too gravely depressed by what
had happened to her and to *Show Boat,* through months of
miserable trouping, to see beyond a single evening's performance and another night's sleepless vigil in her lonely room in
Detroit's Statler Hotel.

So much for the Morgan-*Scandals* mixup and the untrue
account of overnight discovery and sudden stardom that

would be copied in later biographical sketches for more than thirty years.

Now we return, in the summer of 1926, to the minor revue engagement that would eventually bring about a dazzling change in Morgan's existence pattern of thankless theatrical drudgery.

Americana was, for its day, something decidedly different —a topical revue "with ideas." Ziegfeld set out to produce it with the writer J. P. McAvoy, but the two men parted company after an argument concerning two buffaloes the Great Glorifier had purchased over his partner's protests. When J. P. flatly refused to write the two beasts into a skit, Flo abandoned *Americana* and trucked his charges upstate to join a menagerie culled from various *Follies* productions, which he had already installed at his and wife Billie Burke's Hastings-on-Hudson estate.

Now, conceivably, if this contretemps between the two producers had not occurred, Ziegfeld's having failed to recognize Helen's talent while casting *Sally* might have vetoed her warbling in *Americana*. As it was, producer Richard Herndon stepped in to join McAvoy and here, according to another Broadway showman,[6] is what happened to our hapless Helen under the new setup.

Composer Philip Charig, who'd written some special numbers for the review, brought Helen to the Belmont Theater to sing for Herndon, who promptly signed her to play the "prima donna" role in *Americana*. The show tried out at Atlantic City, and the first-night audience's lukewarm reaction there indicated that the songs assigned to Helen were all wrong for her truly unique personality. On receiving her notice the next day, the girl was, of course, devastated, and Charig, who loved her dearly, went to work for her at once, determined to see that she got a break in the show.

When *Americana* returned to New York for a final week's rehearsal, Charig cornered Herndon in desperation to say that

[6] Leonard Sillman, *Here Lies Leonard Sillman* (New York: Citadel Press, 1959), p. 86.

he'd written a special number for Morgan, and that he'd gladly pay her bit player's forty-dollar-a-week salary if Herndon would let her do it.

Herndon pointed out that it was too late for Helen's name to appear in the program, but Charig said that wouldn't matter if only she could have a brief spot in Act Two of *Americana*, so Herndon at last gave in.

Up to this point the story sounds authentic, but from now on Sillman soars into a flight of total fantasy. He has written that Helen "came out and to everybody's surprise sat down at the footlights with her legs dangling in the orchestra pit, turned to the audience, and quietly said, 'My name isn't in the program, but I'd like to sing a song called "Nobody Wants Me." ' She sang it and next day her name was up in lights."

Here again, fiction has taken over from actual fact. As we already know, Morgan sat on an upright piano in the orchestra pit, and nothing happened overnight or otherwise to change her status as an artist until the night Jerome Kern turned up at the Belmont Theater. For example, we learn from a *New York Times* review of *Americana* that "the cast, without possessing any outstanding stars or personalities, generally seems able to meet what requirements are placed upon it."

Neither in the *Times* nor in any other newspaper was Morgan singled out for exceptional praise. Sillman is also incorrect in saying that Helen and the deadpan comedian Charles Butterworth were "made overnight" in the show. Finally, though the *Times* man did describe Butterworth's "banquet scene" as "hilarious," he made no mention of Morgan's success with "Nobody Wants Me."

Plainly, then, there is no more truth in the claim that Helen's name was up in lights on the day after *Americana*'s opening than there is in Miss Farnsworth's tale of her reaching stardom by replacing Helen Hudson on a *Scandals* opening night.

The truth is simply that Helen stayed with *Americana* from its opening on July 26, 1926, until its closing in the last month of that year.

In the late fall, as a result of her success in the little revue, she signed a contract with Joseph Roberts, a well-known nightclub manager, to perform twice nightly in an elegant *boîte* called Helen Morgan's 54th Street Club that may or may not have been backed by gangsters. There is no record of Roberts being directly connected with the underworld, nor would any trouble with mobsters cause him or his *chanteuse*-hostess even a single night's loss of sleep or fearful anxiety.

It was, rather, Helen's new status as a glamorous Broadway personality that got the club in trouble, and the truth about what happened to her at the hands of Prohibition agents working under orders from a vigilant female bigwig in Washington adds up to a far more fascinating story of sudden success and notoriety than any careless theater historian, falling back on the tattered device of overnight stardom, has heretofore recorded.

The new Morgan first made minor headlines in the Manhattan press on January 9, 1927, when a West Side precinct commander named Charles S. Burns, under orders from one Commissioner McLaughlin to enforce a recent 3 A.M. nightclub curfew, sent a patrolman around at 4 A.M. to check out Helen Morgan's 54th Street Club.

Helen was not "at home," but Officer Charles F. Murphy, finding a few diehard patrons still at the tables, served Joe Roberts with a summons to show up on the morning of January 10 at West Side Court.

Miss Morgan was either in bed, or down in Greenwich Village where, as a publicity stunt aimed at helping two unknown young producer friends, she'd been rehearsing some translated horror playlets, under the title *Grand Guignol Repertory*, which would open at the Grove Theater on January 12.

She stayed with this short-lived enterprise for a single week, then began rehearsals for a far more important week's engagement at the Palace Theater.

On January 25 all the papers headlined her opening at the grand old house, and the *Times* man called her a "highly individualized chanteuse" possessed of a "somnolent, smouldering personality with overtones of pathos which give her numbers, even the most banal of them, a certain charm and distinction."

Noting that since appearing in the *Follies* and the *Scandals*, Helen had "done a specialty in *Americana*," the writer mentioned her club operation and ventured a personal assumption: "Earning three incomes, as she will be this week, it is the income tax collectors more than the new curfew law that now give her cause for worry."

Stuff and nonsense, probably. True, with the *Times* black headline blaring "Helen Morgan Among Features at Palace," plus her name in lights at her club and on the Palace's marquee, the composite picture appeared to add up to stunning success, but as for the tax collectors causing her concern in regard to three incomes, the *Times* critic was simply dealing in guesswork.

Morgan was earning just forty dollars a week in *Americana*; in the shoestring-produced *Grand Guignol*, she was probably paid peanuts; her club salary could not yet have reached the amount a theater star could command; and it may be she earned no more than five hundred dollars at the Palace.

After seven tough years in New York, Helen Morgan was definitely on her way, but she was still compelled to look down that lonesome road to stardom, along which—already schooled in frustrating failures and countless disappointments—she may even now have foreseen flash-warning signs that spelled out "dangerous curves ahead."

Meanwhile, this railroad fireman's daughter, ever alert to opportunities for self-improvement, had made a friend in voice coach Estelle Liebling, who had a studio in the Metropolitan Opera House building, and Helen would sometimes drop in there to eavesdrop while Madame worked with an opera student.

On these occasions La Morgan would take from a paper bag a crystal glass, place it between her ear and the thin wall separating the reception room from Liebling's studio, and hum to herself along with the opera pupil. Helen had great respect for Madame, and one day she'd work with the lady on speech and diction, but as of now she was wary of singing lessons. Her voice was small but perfectly pitched, she was already developing a style of her own, and she instinctively feared that professional training might affect the spontaneous, uniquely intimate communication quality she sensed was hers.

However, listening in this manner to Liebling and some student, she figured she might pick up something useful without committing herself to formal training, and if Madame was aware of her young friend's innocent subterfuge, she gave no sign. This girl was a subtly different sort of singer—and in some ways a loner who must be allowed to work out certain personal problems for herself.

Morgan would never have many close women friends. However, after a matinée at the Empire Theater during this winter of 1927 producer Daniel Frohman had introduced her to the singer Raquel Meller, fresh from a triumphant European tour, and despite a language barrier the two women managed to communicate whenever Helen visited backstage.

In this year, too, Morgan sometimes saw the brilliant Ina Claire whom she adored—but now, as ever before, the single important woman in her life was her mother.

Lulu still went with her to producers' and agents' offices, maintaining, "Two pairs of eyes are better than one pair, darling, for reading the fine print in contracts . . ." and the two Morgans frequently shopped together at Arnold Constable's Fifth Avenue store, which was patronized by Eleanor Roosevelt.

Lulu adored the energetic governor's wife, and she would ask on entering the better dress department, "Has Mrs. Roosevelt been in lately?"

The sales girl might reply, "Now let me see, Mrs. Morgan. Why, yes, she was in last Wednesday."

Then Lulu would smile and say, "Eleanor wears sixteen long. May I try on her latest selection, in size fourteen?"

After that, if Lulu was in the store alone, the girl would get a size fourteen and lead the way to a fitting room. But on the days when her famous daughter accompanied Lulu, this proceeding would be halted by autograph-seeking customers and personnel besieging the lovely new celebrity, whose name, winking in lights above her own club and the Palace marquee, had lately become a valuable collectors' item.

This local notoriety constituted a kind of attention that Helen enjoyed, but these late-winter, spring, and summer months of relative peace represented a period of calm before a storm in her life that she'd always think of as Helen Morgan, B.S.; i.e., Before *Show Boat*, the single magnificent production that would at last truly alter her whole existence overnight.

In 1927 (even as today) it was a little-known fact that in the original Broadway *Show Boat* no player was starred, in the sense that no single person's name appeared above the show's title on the New Amsterdam's marquee. There were too many performers in that first great production who rated star billing for Ziegfeld to single out one to be so honored. Yet one day, because of a set of peculiar circumstances, Helen would receive an accolade that no other cast member could ever boast of, when a theater marquee suddenly flashed "Helen Morgan in Ziegfeld's *Show Boat*."

All through her professional life she would be known for her portrayal of Julie Dozier in two Broadway productions, a road show presentation, and a Hollywood film of *Show Boat* —and the two songs that she sang as Julie would serve as her signature until the day she died.

Because of this, any biography of Morgan must become a partial biography of this first breakthrough tragicomedy production that revolutionized American musicals, so let us now turn from Helen's own story to follow *Show Boat* from its genesis through its growth and development to its ultimate realization as a classic theater piece that is still playing somewhere in the world.

3

Genesis and Evolution
of Show Boat

THE STORY OF HOW a casual conversation became an *idée fixe* that grew in an author's mind to become a best-selling novel is no less fascinating than is the complex transition from the novel to the musical play. So here is that story, garnered from various sources and spliced together, for the first time, in a single volume.

One night in New Haven, Connecticut, after a dismal tryout performance of *Old Man Minick*, a play she'd written with George S. Kaufman, the short-story writer and novelist Edna Ferber sat in on a company wake with her play's director and producer, Winthrop Ames.

Half listening, Ferber heard Ames consoling the gloomy cast: "Next time we won't bother with tryouts. We'll charter a show boat and we'll just drift down the rivers, playing the towns as we come to them and we'll never get off the boat. It'll be wonderful."

Ferber, who hadn't realized that any show boats existed, asked Ames what he was talking about. Then, as he described the gaudy vessels that had plied the Mississippi and lesser rivers since the 1860s, this lady from Appleton, Wisconsin— always fascinated by American history—grew intensely excited.

When *Minick* had opened in New York to a satisfactory press, Ferber began a year's research on show boats. She learned that a few still played certain towns along the Mississippi, Missouri, and Ohio rivers, as well as the streams that flowed through North Carolina and the Louisiana bayous. Then one fine day in October 1924 she took a train down to Washington, North Carolina, to visit a show boat.

In the town she hired a black boy to drive her out in a rattling flivver to the dock where the boat was tied up. There she introduced herself to the *James Adams Floating Palace*'s director and leading man, Charles Hunter, who recognized her at once as the author of the popular serialized Emma McChesney stories.

Charlie welcomed her, introduced her to Beulah Hunter, his wife and leading lady, and told her the boat was about to be docked for the winter. He said, however, that he and Beulah would love to have her come down next April to board the boat at Bath, North Carolina, and Edna gladly accepted his invitation.

Ferber kept up her research on show boats all through the winter of 1925. She read up on old river craft, interviewed two show boat troupers, the actor Wallace Ford and a certain *Billboard* editor, then returned in April to North Carolina where, in the old town of Bath, she put up at a mouse-ridden venerable brick rooming house that had served as a governor's mansion during the 1700s.

On her second day in Bath the *Floating Palace* anchored in the Pamlico River and Edna went aboard to join the Hunters, ten other actors, Jo, the black cook, and the pilot.

In her four-day visit Ferber consumed big Southern breakfasts, joined the troupe in late suppers after the evening show, sat in on rehearsals, watched performances, and even sold tickets in the *Palace*'s little box office.

Making small talk with the audiences during intermissions, she noted among the river-folk-crowds occasional faces that might have adorned daguerreotypes and, having already boned up on headstone inscriptions in the moldering Bath churchyard, she began to construct the image and lineage of

Gaylord Ravenal, the handsome gambler-hero of her pro-
jected novel.

On her last day aboard the *Palace*, Ferber took notes for
about eight hours while her generous host reminisced.

Edna begged Hunter to accept a fee for his priceless show
boat and river lore, but Charlie wanted only an autographed
copy of her Pulitzer-prize novel *So Big*, so she posted the
book from New York, accompanying a grateful letter with a
substantial check. Charlie glued the check, souvenir fashion,
to the flyleaf of *So Big*, but broke down and cashed it years
later when the *Floating Palace* suddenly sank, leaving him
temporarily broke.

Ferber spent just one year in creating her novel, which was
serialized and sold to Hollywood before its publication by
Doubleday.

One day composer Jerome Kern read part of it and rang
up the *Times'* drama critic, Alexander Woollcott, to say he'd
found a story from which he could weave the kind of libretto
he'd always been seeking.

When Jerry Kern asked for a letter of introduction to Edna
Ferber, Woollcott, amused, suggested that if he merely called
up and said he was Kern the lady "would hardly slam down
the receiver and barricade the door."

Nevertheless Woollcott wrote the letter and mailed it at
dusk on his way to join Ferber for dinner and the opening
performance of Fred Stone's new play.

Kern also attended the play, and during the first intermission
of *Stepping Stones,* when Woollcott gleefully introduced composer and author, the excited little man, who seemed to Ferber
to have "the most winning smile in the world," cried out, "You
mean this *is* Edna Ferber?"

After that, Woollcott always insisted, his two small-statured,
greatly gifted friends seemed to forget he was present. However, the truth was that Ferber, who'd already heard a rumor
that Kern believed a Broadway musical might be made from
her book, "rather resented the idea." And even as Kern asked
for the dramatic rights to *Show Boat*, she "thought he was

being fantastic" until he explained that he had in mind no old-time conventional revue but rather a musical play that would closely follow the plot of her novel.

On hearing this news, Edna promptly shook hands with her new collaborator and returned to her seat with Woollcott, while Kern sped back, elated, to his own place.

Next day Jerry rang up Oscar Hammerstein and asked him, "How would you like to do a Ziegfeld production with a million-dollar title, *Show Boat*?"

When Hammerstein asked if he meant the new Ferber novel, Kern answered, "Yes, I haven't finished it yet, but I've already bought it from Ferber. Get a copy and read it right away."

Then, hard upon Oscar's cautious inquiry as to whether or not Ziegfeld was enthusiastic, Kern quipped, "He doesn't know anything about it yet," and hung up.

Hammerstein replaced his own receiver, amused but by no means dismayed. As a recent collaborator with Kern on *Sally*, he knew this pixie to be a genius whose reputation had grown without ceasing since 1915, when he'd written memorable music to Guy Bolton's and P. G. Wodehouse's librettos for several well-plotted, intrinsically American musicals that had made big news after their presentation at Manhattan's tiny Princess Theater.

These contemporary shows, unlike the European fairy tale operettas, the Ziegfeld *Follies*, and George White's *Scandals*, had started a trend that would gradually alter the taste of Broadway theatergoers—and Oscar had noted that trend long before he'd met Kern, in May 1924, at Victor Herbert's funeral.

Then, in 1925, producer Charles Dillingham had hired Hammerstein to work with Otto Harbach, a famous musical comedy librettist, on Ziegfeld's *Sally*, for which Kern would write the music, and after an initial trip with Harbach to Kern's place in Bronxville, Oscar decided that Jerry not only knew all about music but "something about everything."

Oscar had gone home that afternoon, "stimulated and

dazed." Later on he'd been overwhelmed by Kern's assertion that—aside from Marilyn Miller's artistry in delivering the hit song "Who?"—*Sally's* commercial success had been due largely to the Harbach-Hammerstein lyrics.

Now, as he stood mulling over the phone call from his friend, Oscar felt no qualms as to Jerry's ability to match his music to any man's libretto. He was just not sure about Flo Ziegfeld's being persuaded to produce a musical play derived from a novel the old master showman probably hadn't read.

After reading and enjoying *Show Boat*, he was relieved within the next few days to learn that Kern had obtained a verbal agreement from Ziegfeld to act as producer.

Ready and eager now to begin creating, the two writers outlined separate adaptations of the book, then found themselves amazingly in agreement on all essential details.

Elated, they wrote a script for Ziegfeld, who promptly took it with him to Hastings-on-Hudson, and asked composer Irving Berlin, a weekend guest, to read it.

Berlin retired to the suite consigned to him and later emerged with a woeful face, pleading, "Don't produce this, Flo. The thing hasn't got a chance, and you'll lose your shirt."

In the ensuing argument Berlin held to his conviction that *Show Boat* would never succeed as a musical, but Mr. Z thought otherwise. He had faith in Ferber, Kern, and Hammerstein, so the two adapters proceeded at full steam, happily unaware that Irving Berlin had done his vehement best to keep Ziegfeld from pursuing a financial gamble that he foresaw as being disastrous.

Oscar and Jerry had fun right from the start with the script and songs of their new musical play. They took a train trip down to Maryland's Eastern Shore to watch a show boat melodrama-oleo program, then settled in to a twenty-four-hour-a-day creative schedule. The two men worked as an unbeatable team, discussing scenes, plot points, chief characterizations, and the ticklish problem of having all the scenes grow out of the script's plot structure in a natural way.

It was a happy time, and Oscar said, remembering, "We

had fallen hopelessly in love with it [and] we couldn't keep
our hands off it. We acted out the scenes together, and planned
the actual direction. We sang to each other. We had ourselves
swooning."[1]

By now the boys had also fallen in love with the character
of Julie Dozier, for whom they'd dreamed up the joyous
"Can't Help Lovin' that Man," and both of them realized that
Julie, described in the book as a sallow-skinned mulatto with
a face rutted by suffering, had to be glamorized for the musical stage.

It was obvious, too, that this brief, three-handkerchief part
would be difficult to cast. Neither Kern nor Hammerstein
could think of a single singing actress who would be quite
right for the role, and indeed, the search for a Julie would be
continued long after every other principal part had been cast.

Meanwhile, as the composers' work went on, the Ziegfeld
building was steadily rising at Sixth Avenue and Fifty-fourth
Street, and Flo had promised to open his splendid new house
with *Show Boat.*

As the time for the opening neared, though, Oscar and Jerry
were still hard at work, so the Ziegfeld Theater opened on
February 2, 1927, with *Rio Rita*, a musical by Harry Tierney
and Guy Bolton, who had been Kern's old Princess Theater
writing partner.

Rio Rita racked up notices that foretold exceptional business, but somehow Jerry Kern couldn't shake a nagging conviction that Ziegfeld, after launching such a lavish production, must be at least flat broke, if not in debt. Consequently
he persuaded Oscar to drive up with him one Sunday to Hastings-on-Hudson for a cards-on-the-table talk with Mr. Z—and
Oscar never forgot that day. As the car turned into the grounds
of Burkeley Crest, they came upon a life-sized copy of a vast
European estate, with a chateau set on a hill and surrounded
by gardens, dovecotes, a glass conservatory, a swimming pool
—and a range for Ziggy's wild animals.

[1] David Ewen, *The World of Jerome Kern* (New York: Holt, Rinehart and Winston, 1966), p. 87.

His guests were met at the mansion's front door by a uniformed butler who showed them into a huge drawing room, then passed them on to a soubrette maid, in lace cap and apron, who led the boys upstairs and through a huge master bedchamber into a lush bathroom where Ziggy, being groomed by his personal barber, called out muffled greetings from beneath a steaming towel.

While the shaving ritual went on, the three men made small talk, then Flo slipped into a brocaded dressing gown and asked his guests to join him in a "snack" that turned out to be a full-course luncheon of thick roast beef with various trimmings, washed down by vintage champagne.

By the time the tipsy partners left Burkeley Crest, the bedazzled Kern, who hadn't dared speak of money, retained no doubts as to Florenz Ziegfeld's current financial status.

Now it seemed strictly up to the boys to finish *their* work in a hurry and get this recalcitrant *Show Boat* spectacle onto the boards.

Nevertheless, the two creators were in for a harrowing series of postponements that began when Ziegfeld insisted he needed a real vacation after producing *Rio Rita* and continued when he advised the composers that he couldn't see closing a box office hit to open *Show Boat* at his theater either in the spring or summer of 1927.

Frustrated and angered by these decisions, Oscar and Jerry toyed with the notion of giving their script and score to Oscar's brother Arthur. Arthur, however, decided to do *Golden Dawn,* another musical of Oscar's, so the partners had to accede to Mr. Z's wishes, and the consequent ten-month postponement of *Show Boat* proved to be a disguised blessing, since the final script was far superior to the boys' first effort.

The team had finished such charmers as "Can't Help Lovin' That Man," "Only Make Believe," and Ravenal's gambling song, "Till Good Luck Comes My Way," before they began rewriting. Then, in a leisurely reappraisal period, the two decided they needed a number to make the theater audience conscious, as readers of the novel had been, of the mighty Mississippi's importance as a sort of protagonist. So they wrote

a song for a nonsituation spot in Act One, to be sung by a
dock worker named Joe, that both writers suddenly realized
was something very special indeed.

One afternoon near dusk Jerry dropped in at Edna Ferber's
apartment to play and sing "Ol' Man River" for her, and Edna
later reported that her hair "stood on end" as she wept and
"breathed like a heroine in a melodrama."[2]

Meanwhile, back at the ranch (quite literally the Ziegfeld
ranch on Billie Burke Island northeast of Quebec), the seemingly dilatory producer was not idling after all.

Up there in the woods Mr. Z was working with his New
York production staff by remote control, and here's how Billie
Burke Ziegfield described those activities: ". . . strange as it
may seem, considering the loveliness and sentiment of that most
beautiful of all musical plays, Flo produced it almost entirely
on Western Union blanks. Woods or no woods, the telegrams
flowed in steady staccato, delivered at who knows what cost."[3]

Then, in the early summer, Kern discovered his Julie, and
by the time Ziegfeld was ready to draw up a contract with
Helen Morgan, *she* had drawn up a contract with Arthur
Benton, a personal representative who would be far more
positive than she about assessing her monetary worth as an
artist.

Benton might best have been described as a typical "ordinary man" of average height with salt-and-pepper hair, whose
mild manner belied considerable business acumen coupled
with an innate integrity that endeared him to such loyal clients as Laurette Taylor, Ina Claire, Irene Bordoni, Alice
Brady, Mary Eaton, and that self-styled "great man," W. C.
Fields.

Benton had no problem in negotiating, with the ever-gener-
ous Ziegfeld, a five-hundred-dollar weekly contract for his new

---

[2] Edna Ferber, *A Peculiar Treasure* (New York: Garden City Publishers, 1939), p. 299.

[3] Billie Burke, with Cameron Shipp, *With a Feather on My Nose*
(New York: Appleton-Century-Crofts, Inc., 1949), p. 186.

client, but Helen would soon learn that he could demand of tougher producers at the height of her nightclub career, a yearly sum for her services that could match the annual earnings of any other topflight Broadway entertainer.

Before half a year had passed, Morgan would be on her way to the top, but now, in the summer of 1927, being far less assured than Kern of her potentialities as Julie, she was not resentful when Edna Ferber told her one day, "My dear, since you've had no stage experience except in revues, you ought to go to a good dramatic coach for some work on your speaking voice."

Ferber sent her to see Ina Claire, whom Helen had met backstage in 1918 when the soignée comedienne was starring in *Ode to Liberty*, and Ina recommended her own coach, Frances Robinson Duff, a regal lady whose name was a household word with actors.

Helen dutifully enrolled in a class with other aspiring young thespians at Mrs. Duff's august studio, but she took just five lessons and departed after participating in one of Madame's Friday afternoon showcase sessions for Broadway producers and directors.

Asked why she'd reneged on finishing the culture course, Miss Morgan explained: "My God, no matter what kind of part they were trying to play—scrubwoman, prostitute, or society dame—all those gals talked as if they'd been raised in an old New York family. Also, exactly like Miss Duff, and so much like each other you could hardly tell 'em apart."

On her own, then, Miss Morgan went to her friend, Miss Estelle Liebling, at the Metropolitan Opera House studios, and there turned the speaking voice trick to her own and Miss Ferber's satisfaction. But still, after being especially chosen by Kern to play Julie Dozier—she was forced to pass muster on another surprising count.

One day she went to Ziegfeld's office, at his request, where Ferber and Flo told her, "Take off your shoes and stockings, honey. Now walk all the way to the wall and back the way Julie would."

Puzzled, Helen tripped to the wall, and on her return trek Julie's creator and *Show Boat*'s production head beamed evident approval.

"All right," said Helen a little testily, "now that I've done what you asked, would you mind telling me what that was all about?"

Well, it seems this pair of perfectionists had the idea that a proud mulatto walks with her head and breasts up, propelling her body from the hips—and damned if Helen Morgan hadn't been walking that way all her life.

Quietly amused, she left the Ziegfeld Theater office pondering the possibility of there having been a distant dusky ancestor somewhere in her family tree, but since Tom's and Lulu's people had been pure Irish since the years of the potato famine, Helen concluded that walking like an ideal Julie was, for her, something that just came naturally.

By this time, though she was a good friend of Kern's, Morgan hadn't met Hammerstein, who appeared on the first day of rehearsals at the New Amsterdam Theater to read all the uncast parts and pinch-hit for the show's director who hadn't yet been selected.

Helen was much taken with this soft-voiced, self-effacing, blunt-featured fellow with dark, long-lashed eyes, and after watching him go quietly about his business, she asked Ziegfeld if a part couldn't be found for this attractive man who seemed to be a kind of jack-of-all-trades.

On hearing who Oscar was, Morgan felt like a fool, but she still couldn't keep her admiring glance off that gentle face —and Oscar, who soon began, with Kern's help, to take over as *Show Boat*'s official director, became increasingly aware of the lady's interest in him.

Now certain people who were around the New Amsterdam at this time believed that nothing serious happened between Hammerstein and Helen because of his marital status, but there was no doubt about the warmth of Oscar's feeling for her. Having watched with amazement the steadily growing characterization of Julie in the hands of this woman who'd never played a dramatic part before, he said, "Everything she did was exactly right. Her instincts were sure. Nobody had to tell her how to move, gesture, or even put over a song. She behaved like a veteran."

At the end of an afternoon's rehearsal Oscar would always be solicitous of Helen, asking if he could drive her home, and when she'd say, "Oh, Oscar, you don't have to go out of your way for me," he would answer stoutly, "Sweetheart, there's no such thing as going out of my way for you."

Later, as Helen let herself into the Fifty-fourth Street apartment, Lulu would call out, "Honey, that was Oscar's car at the curb *again*, wasn't it? I've got such a wonderful cheese and pineapple pie [or chocolate cake or streudel] in the oven. Why didn't you ask him in?"

And Helen's answer to that would seldom vary from the ritualistic reply, "Well, Mama, you know Oscar has such a long drive out to Long Island."

Morgan was a stunning young woman, and Hammerstein was certainly flattered by her feeling for him, but these two people were more conventional than showpeople often are, so it does seem evident that no illicit relationship ever developed between them.

Now—chiefly because of a disagreement between Ziegfeld and the writers of *Show Boat* regarding a scene in which Helen Morgan appeared—the time has come to give a brief synopsis of the novel, and to touch on certain differences between Ferber's book and the play script.

The book's substantial plot unfolds in the following fashion: Captain Andy Hawks, who owns the *Cotton Blossom Floating Palace,* has a granite-willed ex-schoolteacher wife named Parthenia (Parthy) Ann and a daughter, born on a stormy night on the Mississippi, named Magnolia.

The little girl loves the troupe's indolent, gold-skinned, carelessly lovely Julie Dozier, who is married to Steve Baker, the troupe's leading man. On the day the *Cotton Blossom* docks at Lemoyne, Mississippi, where Julie was born, the actress takes sick and announces that she'll be unable to play that night.

Late in the afternoon, when the redneck local sheriff is spied crossing the levee, Steve seizes Julie's hand, cuts the tip of her forefinger with his pocket knife, and sucks the blood.

Ten minutes later, when the sheriff accuses him of being a white man married to a "nigger," Steve says he has Negro blood in him and anybody present can swear to it. The sheriff leaves, convinced, warning Cap'n Andy not to give his show that night, since the troupe is now deep in the bigoted South. Next day, at a town called Xenia, Steve and Julie are forced to leave the troupe, for, naturally, as the show boat steams downriver word will spread like wildfire all the way to New Orleans that Cap'n Andy's company has for a long time included a white man married to a mulatto wench.

Julie tries to get off the docks before Magnolia finds out she's gone, but Magnolia runs after her and Julie breaks down as she kneels in the dusty road, embracing the little girl.

Time passes and Magnolia, at fifteen, replacing the ingenue Elly Schultz, who has run off with another man, becomes a river favorite. At New Orleans the ingenue's husband, Frank, hearing that his wife's lover has deserted her in Little Rock, leaves the boat to go to her, but not before he has recommended a handsome fellow he'd met on the wharf who claimed to have done some acting. Cap'n Andy picks him out with binoculars—an elegantly dressed, slim man, leaning against a packing case on the wharf; then, being advised by his wife to go ashore and talk to the stranger, he cries, "Him! Why, I couldn't go up and talk to him about acting on no show boat. He's a gentleman."

Parthy Ann takes a look through the glasses, announcing, "He may be a gentleman. But nobody feels a gentleman with a crack in his shoe, and he's got one."

So Andy goes down to the wharf to interview the gentleman, who, after spotting Magnolia on the *Cotton Blossom*'s upper deck, learns that she is Andy's daughter and the troupe's leading lady as well. Thus it comes to pass that Gaylord Ravenal, gentleman gambler, comes aboard the boat to play romantic leads, falls in love with Magnolia, and, finally, despite Parthy Ann's disapproval, maneuvers her off the boat one day at Paducah, Kentucky, and marries her. He returns to the boat with Magnolia to brave his new mother-in-law's excessive wrath and receive Andy's delighted congratulations.

Within a year the Ravenals have a baby, born on the Mississippi at a place near Kentucky, Illinois, and Missouri, who is named with the first letters of the three states—K-I-M—Kim. When Kim is four years old, Cap'n Andy is swept overboard in a storm, Parthy Ann takes over the *Cotton Blossom*'s management, and Ravenal, whom she has always treated coldly, tells his wife she must now choose between him and her mother.

Magnolia chooses him, and the pair go to Chicago where Magnolia endures the mercurial existence of a gambler's wife, moving from such posh places as the Sherman House, when Gay runs out of luck, to a shabby, small hotel on Ontario Street.

When Kim is ten, Magnolia places her in a convent school. Then, during a bad time when the Ravenals are staying at the cheap hotel, Parthy Ann writes that she is coming to Chicago to visit them. Horrified, Ravenal goes out, gets drunk, and returns with two thousand dollars. He has borrowed a grand from a Clark Street madam named Hetty Chilson and parlayed it into two at roulette.

The next morning, while he is sleeping, Magnolia goes to Hetty Chilson's whorehouse to return the money. The madam summons her assistant, whom she calls Julie, to write a receipt —and suddenly in the hall's dim light, the tall, gray-haired woman in black silk recognizes Magnolia. She panics and rushes up the stairs out of sight as Magnolia cries, just as she did years before on the day of parting at Xenia, "Julie, wait for me."

Now, at the end of the novel, Ravenal leaves Magnolia, who goes to work at the Masonic Roof, singing the Negro songs she had learned on the Mississippi. Kim grows up and becomes an actress. When Parthy Ann dies, Magnolia returns to the *Cotton Blossom* to live out her last years on the river she has always fearfully loved.

So much for *Show Boat* as a novel. In the play script there is no whorehouse scene. Magnolia goes to a place called the Trocadero to audition, and Julie, who is singing there, hearing her voice, discreetly vanishes, leaving the stage (and her job) to Magnolia.

Well, we already know that Kern had made up his mind to give his long-cherished "Bill" to Morgan, but it seems that Ziegfeld objected to the use of the song on the ground that it was not an integral part of a *Show Boat* situation.

At the start of rehearsals Helen had only two scenes on the *Cotton Blossom*, and the single song "Can't Help Lovin' That Man."

Then one afternoon the big wheels went into a huddled discussion as to how to get her back onstage for a final scene off the boat and what precisely to do about an encounter between Julie and Magnolia—which resulted in a decision to have Julie Dozier sing "My Bill" in a rehearsal scene at the Chicago Trocadero, before Magnolia's arrival to audition there. And so Helen Morgan was at last allowed to do the one song in *Show Boat* that would always bring down the house.

4

Show Boat *Opens to* *Paeans of Praise*

REHEARSALS FOR *Show Boat* HAD BEGUN at the New Amsterdam around the first of October, and there seems never to have been a happier, harder working company. Edna Ferber, who had a play of hers and George Kaufman's called *The Royal Family* in rehearsal at the Plymouth on West Forty-fourth Street, has told, in her autobiography, *A Peculiar Treasure*, what it was like to leave that theater to look in on *Show Boat* at the New Amsterdam. She would find the dance director supervising one group; the music director, another; and someone going over dialogue and business in a third section.

In a dark corner of the big stage Charley Winninger would be doing full body flips, while the dance team of Eva Puck and Sam White rehearsed a cakewalk. The chorus girls would be doing a tricky routine even as Kern, at the piano, conferred with Norma Terris or Howard Marsh, and Hammerstein instructed Edna May Oliver.

Then as the rehearsal slumped a bit, Ziegfeld would invariably turn up yelling, "What the hell's this? You're dragging around like a lot of corpses. If you let down in rehearsal, you'll do the same thing a week after we've opened. Any of you boys and girls too tired to go on please get out. Go home! And stay there."

But nobody minded because they knew Ziggy didn't really mean to be brutal, and even in the last week before the Washington opening the company remained cheerful, slaving twenty hours at a stretch.

Show Boat opened at the National Theater in Washington, D.C., on November 15, 1927, for a fortnight's run.

Edna Ferber sat second row center, between Kern and Hammerstein, thrilled as always by that breathless moment when the house lights faded out before the heavy abestos curtain's silent ascension.

All through the gorgeous spectacle Florenz Ziegfeld sat tensely beside his general manager, Stanley Sharpe, until that moment in the Trocadero scene when Helen Morgan finished "My Bill" to unrestrained applause. Then the old pro reached out, grasped his companion's arm, and exulted, "Stanley, the show is in."

Magnolia Ravenal was by rights *Show Boat*'s leading feminine role, but Julie Dozier, in the person of Helen Morgan, singing her one-man, one-woman song, had tonight taken the whole house, and (potentially) the capital city, by storm.

The curtain had gone up at eight-fifteen. It descended finally at half an hour past midnight, and not a single person in the mesmerized audience had left the National Theater.

Backstage after the play, Helen Morgan's dressing room was packed with admirers, in and out of "the business," eager to see, touch, and congratulate this woman who had so moved them as Julie Dozier.

Norma Terris, perfectly cast as Magnolia, had her admirers too, but there was no mistaking from this night forward who would be considered the star of *Show Boat*.

Rightfully, because of her own fine work and the length of her part, that accolade belonged to Norma Terris—and when the mad rush for Morgan occurred, she undoubtedly felt some qualms of jealous resentment, but it would not have behooved her to voice them. The silver star was affixed to her dressing room door—and also, Miss Morgan had just three scenes in *Show Boat*. Therefore, if she'd reached out in the relatively minor role of Julie to cup the collective heart of an audience in her hand, well . . . Kismet, and that's show business, baby.

Besides, in the play Magnolia adored Julie—and somehow,

in real life, it was hard to resent or dislike Helen Morgan, whose ingrained sincere humility as an artist was unmistakably evident.

The show was now considerably shortened and the tired cast that night took its bows, bone-weary yet tensely elated as the curtain rose and fell, time and time again.

Word-of-mouth raves sped through Washington overnight, and in the morning, even before nine o'clock, a line of people stood in the rain, circling past the unopened box office, around the block, and back to the National's marquee.

Kern and Hammerstein continued to cut for two weeks in Washington, and even after the opening at the Erlanger Theater in Philadelphia on December 5.

Show Boat was back in Manhattan by mid-December, and somehow, despite rehearsals, Helen Morgan managed to find time for her Christmas shopping. Christmas had always been for her a sentimental season in which she waxed prodigally generous with Lulu and special friends, as well as the cast and crew of any show in which she was working.

This year, of course, her list included the Chez Morgan personnel, and everyone there from the manager and the maître d' to the smallest busboy and the lowliest restroom attendant would be remembered.

Presents for the male and female personnel (distinctive cravats and expensive compacts) would be uniform, but the gifts for Lulu and a few close associates required careful selection.

This year, not only at Arnold Constable's and Saks but also at Macy's and Gimbels, Miss Morgan found herself surrounded, scribbling autographs, while Lulu stood to one side, proudly watching. Here was fame, at last, and both the Morgans exulted, making the most of it. This year the holidays would be a time of lavish celebration and fervent thanks to God for the big break that had finally come.

On Christmas Eve the real spruce tree in the club's main room glowed with old-fashioned wax tapers. There were gaily wrapped presents, piled beneath the tree's redolent branches, and the whole place seemed festive enough, yet on this night, just after she had handed out the gifts, Miss Morgan returned from a trip to the ladies' lounge, sat down at the table with friends, and burst into tears.

When a chorus of voices begged to know what was the matter, she took a big gulp of brandy, sobbing, "That poor woman in there has to work tonight when she ought to be at home with her family."

More than likely recalling a Christmas Eve when Lulu, working late at a railroad lunchroom, hadn't reached home until midnight, Helen wept afresh, while her companions sought to console her. Then she dried her eyes, climbed up on the Steinway, and sang her tremulous, haunting songs.

Later, she wove her somewhat unsteady way back to the powder room, slipped a hundred-dollar bill into the attendant's hand, and fled before the astonished woman could thank her.

Helen felt somehow depressed on this Christmas Eve, but still she realized she had reason to be truly grateful. *Show Boat*, even before its opening in Manhattan was already big news on Broadway. Chez Morgan, as one of the most exclusive nightclubs in town, was doing great business and New Year's Eve reservations would doubtless exceed capacity. She had no apparent reason for feeling apprehensive—but then, there had been the tough weeks out of town with *Show Boat*, plus the past week's rehearsals, and what with the New Amsterdam opening only two days off, perhaps it was natural enough that she couldn't quite shake a sense of impending disaster.

On *Show Boat*'s opening night in New York, December 27, the script was still half an hour too long. As it turned out, that didn't matter. The capacity audience, ranging from formally dressed first-nighters to the very last row of earnest theatergoers in the peanut gallery, blistered their palms and raised the New Amsterdam's roof beams with countless bravos.

In the morning all the reviewers lifted their voices in a collective paean of praise.

Robert Garland called the production "an American masterpiece." Stephen Rathbun said, "From any angle, *Show Boat* deserves the highest praise."

Brooks Atkinson and Percy Hammond, first-string critics of the *Times* and the *Tribune*, respectively, had decided to cover the opening of Phillip Barry's *Paris Bound*. But again, as things turned out, nobody cared. In the *Times* a young man named John Byram praised Kern and Hammerstein for their strict adherence to Ferber's story and their "lilting and satisfactory score," then joyously lilted himself, "*Show Boat* is just about the best musical piece ever to arrive under Mr. Ziegfeld's silken gonfalon." And Richard Watts, Jr., in the *Trib,* hailed the production as "a triumph, a beautiful example of musical comedy."

The *Times* man singled out for exceptional praise Charles Winninger as Cap'n Andy and Norma Terris as Magnolia. Then, proving himself forever shortsighted, he failed to praise the characterization of Julie Dozier, merely observing, "Helen Morgan, who is among the town's most adept saleswomen, was Julie, and purveyed two numbers in her distinctive style."

More than a fortnight after the opening Mr. Atkinson reviewed the play for the *Times*. Praising the "faithful adaptation" and the "enchanting score," he called *Show Boat* "an epochal work." Yet even he, while lauding Charles Winninger, Edna May Oliver as Parthy Ann, and the dance team of Eva Puck and Sammy White, contented himself with observing, "Helen Morgan [is] the woman pursued by fate."

And pursued by fate she would soon be, in more ways than one. She had ample reason to be depressed by the niggardly mentions she'd gotten in New York's leading newspapers—and something worse was about to happen to her—for here she was, after seven years on Broadway, still seeking theatrical stardom. On the other side of the coin something remarkably good that neither she nor the newsmen could have foreseen was about to happen to her, too, for in less than a month plain folks from Dubuque, Des Moines, Jersey City, and all points north, south, east, and west in America would be badgering brokers for tickets, not to Mr. Ziegfeld's *Show Boat* but to "that new musical—you know, the one where the dark-haired woman sits on the piano and sings about her Bill."

What she did with "Can't Help Lovin' That Man" and "My Bill" amounted to a phenomenon that no one, least of all herself, could ever explain. Night after night when she was "on" doing those songs, crew members, cast principals and chorus people stood breathless in the wings, watching and listening while she made her unfailing magic. They were there for the bloodletting scene as well, and time and time again someone leaving the wings would marvel, "Good Lord, to think she can sing and *act* like that, when she never had a lesson in her life."

The silver insignia remained on the door of Miss Terris's dressing room, but there was no mistaking the special, indefinable quality emanating from this woman who'd become, with a single dramatic singing role, a star of the first magnitude.

5

Trouble with the Feds

ON THURSDAY, DECEMBER 29, at Chez Morgan, midnight gave way without undue incident to the early hours of an old year's new day. The place was packed, the eight-piece orchestra was swinging, and Helen Morgan, wearing black velvet and her strand of matchless pearls, had already finished her first show.

Now the white light of the spot dimmed out on her face as she slid off the piano to join some newspaper men at the bar.

While ordering drinks for the boys, she failed to notice two nondescript patrons who suddenly rose from a table and left the room.

These men walked down the carpeted stairs of the club to the iron-grilled front door. They dragged its uniformed guardian onto the sidewalk, while a moustached, heavy-set citizen, flanked by twenty-five unprepossessing minions, entered the club. Upstairs a man stood in the middle of the big room, shouting "This place is in the hands of Federal officers. You will all remain seated until you are told what to do."

Then, while the heavy-set citizen, Prohibition Administrator Maurice Campbell, took over, bellowing orders, various members of his gang scurried to cover the exits. Others plodded about among the tables, taking names and addresses of more than two hundred patrons, then drove them off to the cloakroom with orders to claim their hats and coats and get out.

Speechless, scarcely able to believe her eyes, Helen Morgan

stood staring while Maurice Campbell's vandals seized bottles from beneath and on top of tables, ransacked deserted booths, and searched other suspect places behind and in front of the bar.

They came up with a haul that included nine quarts of champagne, eight quarts of scotch, two of gin, and two of rye; one "bottle" each of gin, Benedictine, and Bacardi rum; two and one-half flagons of cognac; and a single pint of champagne. Then, with the gleeful ardor of small boys invading an empty, defenseless house, Campbell and his cohorts proceeded, as Helen and eight scared waiters were urged down the stairs, about their grisly work of senseless destruction.[1]

While Miss Morgan and her companions rode down to the West Thirtieth Street precinct, the FBI's dry agents wrecked the Chez Morgan bar, smashed glassware, shredded lace curtains and tapestries, destroyed electrical fixtures and tore out the plumbing in the men's and women's lounges.

Outside, on West Fifty-second Street, hundreds of irate people, in cars and on the sidewalks, waited appalled for the second act in a nightmare tragicomedy—and all at once it began.

Down the stairs in squads trudged Campbell's agents and fifteen warehousemen, carrying tables, chairs, linen, silverware, lamps, music racks, and wall lighting fixtures.

Lastly, a half-dozen huskies came out with Helen's piano, while two other oafs staggered under the weight of her glittering, degraded Yuletide tree—and suddenly, as these items were being loaded into warehouse trucks, all the watching people found a collective voice. Women in sables and mink, swarms of less affluent citizens in business clothes, scrubwomen, night watchmen, and janitors hissed and booed Major Campbell, his clumsy fellow agents, and the fifteen warehouse movers.

Catcalls, curses, and Bronx cheers mingled with the frantic blaring of automobile horns as the people who loved Helen

[1] As a former reporter and press agent, Campbell, who had doubtless interviewed Morgan and drunk at her expense, must have avoided any direct confrontation with her.

Morgan stormed their outraged disapproval of a holocaust unequaled in the annals of an eight-year endurance contest between trigger-happy bootleggers and gun-toting, crooked dry agents in a farce called Prohibition enforcement.

Down at the precinct house, "Helen Morgan, Actress, Home Address: 65 West 54th Street" was booked, fingerprinted, and locked up, along with her fellow employees.

Her attorney, J. Arthur Adler, arrived posthaste to rescue and reassure his terrified lady huddled in mink behind the bars of a cell. Then, even as he worked toward her release and the waiters', Adler told it to the press like it was: "The damage to Chez Morgan, which amounts to $75,000, is largely the result of malicious mischief."

He pointed out that the club's owners, in addition to damaged property and fixtures, would suffer a huge monetary loss as a result of canceled New Year's Eve reservations, not to mention the possibility that the wrecked club would be dark for months after the start of 1928, if not forever.

Angrily the lawyer denied that his beautiful, talented client owned any part of Chez Morgan. He swore that she was just "a high-class entertainer," then rapped out: "This is not the time for me to go into the matter of wilful destruction, but I hereby make formal demand for the return of all furniture, miscellaneous articles, electric lighting apparatus, and what not, which were taken without warrant, and I call upon the Government representatives to see that they are returned forthwith."[2]

Seething inside and out, Adler kept on working like a Trojan on his clients' behalf, but it was almost 5:30 A.M. before he was allowed to effect Helen's and the waiters' releases, at a bail fee of one thousand dollars per person.

Helen got little sleep before she was forced to return to the precinct house on New Year's Eve at three P.M. to be arraigned with the waiters on a warrant that charged them not with violating the Volstead Act but with "being parties to a scheme to remove and conceal from Federal officers, with intent to

[2] *New York Times*, 31 December 1927, p. 19.

escape revenue and defraud the Government of such pay-
ment," the scanty stock of liquors confiscated by Campbell.

Now, in distant retrospect, this flimsy unpaid-government-
tax excuse for wrecking Chez Morgan seems unnecessarily
devious, *unless* Major Campbell had theretofore been unable to
prove that proprietor Joseph Roberts was selling and serving
booze he'd bought from bootleggers.

Apparently this was true, since in regard to the seizure of
liquor found at the club the *New York Times* reported U.S.
Attorney Robert B. Watts as claiming that the raiding and
wrecking were justified by Section 3452 of the Revenue Act,
which made "the possession of property of any sort and
unpaid, grounds for seizure."

The warrant, Watts said, carried a fine of five hundred
dollars plus double the amount of tax money due on the
impounded booze. Furthermore, Section 3453 could be
invoked, giving Campbell the right to seize *all* property on
any premises where contraband goods might be found.

In presenting these statistics, the *Times* reporter who wrote
an article for Saturday's paper, coolly observed that "as far as
could be learned," Campbell and his zealous men had seized
at Chez Morgan only liquors "which might have been the
property of the guests," thus surely posing the question of
whether or not the Chez Morgan's owners could lawfully be
held responsible for taxes on booze that perhaps *they* hadn't
bought.

On this evening, after her arraignment, Helen Morgan went
down as usual to the New Amsterdam Theater, where she was
greeted with sympathetic cries and such indignant outbursts
as, "It's just a shame and an outrage, *that's* what it is, darling."

Helen seemed calm on the surface, but actually the raid
and wrecking of her club, not to mention the hours spent
behind bars, would leave her with only spasmodic impressions
of all that had happened between 1:30 and 5:30 A.M. on
Friday, December 31.

In later years, recalling as best she could the mad events of that nightmare four-hour stretch, she would say, "I was at the bar, buying drinks for a couple of newspaper fellows, when *they* walked in and took over. I remember Campbell's leading Jimmy Walker out through the alley, and after that not much —except how those bastards treated poor Francis X. and his friends."

She would go on then to tell how a pair of dry agents had stopped at the table where Francis X. Mahoney, a former circus clown who played Rubber Face in *Show Boat,* sat surrounded by gay boys, and gruffly ordered the group to turn their pockets inside out, then marched each boy who was toting a powder puff "straight off to the black Maria."

And always she would say, "You know, that old major belongs to the family that owns the two most popular theatrical mortuaries in town, and, honey, all I ask is, when I die, don't let *anybody* pack me off to a Campbell's funeral parlor."

She had, of course, a victim's right to despise the major, but the truth of the matter was (as she would discover in 1928) that the publicity-hungry Campbell would never be able to qualify as her most vehement, persistent, relentless persecutor.

That shabby distinction would soon be revealed as belonging to a vigilant individual in Washington, D. C., who was already scheming to plague Helen in the new year with further raids, and far more subtle agents than Major Campbell.

This enemy was a woman named Mabel Walker Willebrandt, who rejoiced in the title of "assistant attorney general of the United States, in charge of cases under the Prohibition laws and the Bureau of Federal Prisons."

In the words of Stanley Walker, a shrewdly observant historian of the 1920s, "Mrs. Willebrandt was determined to put the lovely, dreamy Helen out of business," and this was passing strange indeed, inasmuch as she had distinguished herself as a Los Angeles lawyer a few years back, in about two thousand cases, as a dauntless defender of women.

Her ascension to power as a Prohibition bigwig is more easily understandable inasmuch as she had been born and raised in the town of Woodsdale in the bone-dry state of Kansas of a bone-dry father who owned and edited a weekly county newspaper.

Mabel was thirty-eight years old in 1927, and she had worked without ceasing in Washington, since September 27, 1921, to uphold the Eighteenth Amendment. One perceptive newsman described her as "deft and inscrutable," which she undoubtedly was. She also was keenly perceptive, and after less than half a year in Washington she announced that hundreds of dry agents who'd secured their ill-paid jobs through "political pull" had no more "honesty and integrity" than bootleggers, nor were "scores" of these men more fit to enforce U.S. government laws and carry guns than "the notorious bandit, Jesse James."

It took her nearly six years to catch wise on another score, but finally, in 1928, she decided that any smart manager, host, or hostess of a first-class nightclub or speakeasy could spot the average "dry" agent on sight. And having reached this conclusion, she told herself, "Mabel, some changes must now be made."

Thus, as the changing old order gave way to the new, the late 1920s model Prohibition enforcement official took on some class. He or she, dressed for an evening out in formal black, also had to exude an air of gentility and sufficient surface culture to disarm any nightclub manager, maître d', or top entertainment personality in all Manhattan.

And Mabel Walker Willebrandt did most definitely mean Manhattan. For, even though a number of major American cities including the nation's capital could boast speakeasies and clubs aplenty, this lady's big guns were trained on Jimmy Walker's fun town, where Tammany Hall and Governor Alfred E. Smith, her two most despised objectives, must be attacked.

Mabel had massive plans in the making, but meanwhile the show must go on, so Major Campbell and company, obeying orders and oozing the new urbanity, managed a mild raid at the popular Jungle club, with only four arrests and no destruction of property.

Also meanwhile (and perhaps this had something to do with the Jungle Club's good fortune), attorney J. Arthur Adler, representing Chez Morgan, its exiled singing star, and four waiters, pursued with U.S. Attorney Charles H. Tuttle negotiations resulting in Tuttle's admission that Major Campbell's destruction of Chez Morgan had been perpetrated "without due process of law."

On the last day of February 1928 a federal judge named Mack cleared Helen Morgan of all charges and ordered that the furnishings and fixtures of the club that bore her name be returned. Then the *Times* felt moved to report that inasmuch as Major Campbell, in attempting to justify his actions, had cited an internal revenue statute half a century old, his Washington "superiors" had "suggested" to him that he'd do better in the future "to confine his activities to enforcing more recent statutes." The *Times* man also added that Campbell had "found himself in an embarrassing position" because his Chez Morgan raid had been perpetrated "without due process of law."

This was true, of course, but Campbell *was* acting under orders from Mabel Walker Willebrandt to harass "the lovely dreamy Helen" whom Mabel "intended to put out of business."

This intention would become increasingly evident in 1928, but the baffling question remains: why Helen, rather than the reigning nightclub queen, Miss Texas Guinan, whose "butter and egg men" customers and Wall Street brokers patrons were nightly contributing baskets of folding green to the coffers of her gangster backers, who certainly included Larry Fay, known as "the Racketeer," and probably the sinister gambler-mobster Arnold Rothstein?

Why had Campbell been ordered to descend at Christmas time on the elegant Chez Morgan and its ladylike hostess rather than on the 300 Club, where the rambunctious Miss Guinan unfailingly greeted each arriving party with her raucous trademark cry, "Hello, suckers!" and brought on her line of near-naked, talentless chorines, bawling, "Come on, let's give these little girls a great big hand!"

There may have been at least two reasons why Campbell was told to bypass the 300 Club on his way to tear up the Chez Morgan. First, because such well-known mobsters as Fay and Rothstein were no ginks to fool around with, whereas nobody seemed to know whether or not Chez Morgan's anonymous backers had underworld connections. Or because the arrest and conviction of the frequently handcuffed Tex Guinan would create no such headline publicity as Washington's Mrs. Willebrandt could count on through the temporary jailing and arraignment of Helen Morgan, the town's most talented torch singer who had recently become the sensational highlight of *Show Boat*.

Whichever reason was correct (and one of them surely was), the personalities of Morgan and Guinan, as well as the atmospheres of their clubs, present intriguing comparisons.

In the first place, no pair of topflight personalities in an identical racket could have been less alike.

Neither in the press of the late 1920s nor in any book on the Prohibition era was Helen Morgan ever dubbed "Queen of the Nightclubs," nor would this soft-spoken, naturally beautiful, talented, publicity-shunning railroad fireman's daughter have ever wished to compete for that dubious title with Texas Guinan, the loud-mouthed, garishly painted Texas rancher's offspring who, next to the steady ring of a cash register, loved nothing so much as being dubbed by her "suckers" and the tabloid columnists as the New York nightclub world's "most sensational personality."

According to at least two historians of the twenties, Guinan was a good enough scout, liked by gangsters, cops, her customers, and even her "little girls," whom she is said to have tried to protect from pawing patrons; but culture-wise, let us face it: Nancy Astor she wasn't. She was said to be openhanded with friends, but she has left no indisputable record, as has Helen Morgan, of an awesome generosity that transcended even reason and cautious forethought for tomorrow.

Guinan had reached Broadway via the hard route, and she might well have been the prototype of that entertainer-heroine in Damon Runyon's story *The Big Street* who told her black maid, "Believe me, Ruby, a girl's best friend is a dollar."

Nevertheless, dissimilar as they were, Helen and Tex were good friends, so here is a close up of Mary Louise Cecilia Guinan.

At fourteen, this ambitious romp of the rancho won a singing scholarship that took her to a Chicago conservatory where she seems not to have lingered overlong. Down the years she rode a bronco in a one-ring circus, trouped in small-time vaudeville, and made some two-reel Western silent films for which she came to be known temporarily as "the female Bill (William S.) Hart."

While appearing without fanfare in a show at New York's Winter Garden in 1923, Guinan went out one night to the Cafe des Beaux Arts. The place was downright dreary, so Guinan decided to stir up a bit of dust. She ripped off a hoarse-voiced number to a round of applause, then topped the song with a few broad wisecracks that kept the customers chortling. The Beaux Arts manager promptly hired her as a femme M.C., and in no time at all the grub from the nowhere Winter Garden show (which she'd deserted) emerged as the gaudiest nightmoth to be found in any Manhattan hotspot ranging from the Battery region to the farthest water hole up in Harlem.

Within a year after her Beaux Arts debut Larry Fay hired Tex to pack the suckers in at his El Fey Club, and after a time she formed a partnership with Fay, moving at the will of the dry agents from one padlocked joint to another until she reached the flourishing 300 Club in 1927.

So much for Guinan, in closeup. Now, as to Larry Fay and Arnold Rothstein—Larry "the Racketeer," for all his outward resemblance to Runyon's tall, thin, equine-visaged anti-hero "Harry the Horse," was no murderer. Fay, who came out of Hell's Kitchen, graduated from a teenager's job as a bundle wrapper to driving a single cab, which he parlayed through a hundred-to-one shot on a racehorse named Scotch Verdict into a fleet of cabs driven by such trustworthy old acquaintances as ex-convicts and overage prize fighters.

Fay had a record of forty-six summonses and arrests, all for private quarrels, lawsuits, and such minor offenses as sassing traffic cops, but this tall thin character who looked, in his uniform of tailored black suit, spotless white shirt, black tie, and broad-brimmed black hat, like the traditional movie image of a prime-time gentleman gangster, never killed anybody.

With Arnold Rothstein, who is said to have backed "some" of the clubs over which Tex presided, and perhaps the 300, it was another thing entirely. This mobster, gambler, and usurer had more than one bodyguard, including the sadistic, trigger-happy hoodlum Legs Diamond, who seems to have slaughtered quite a few big winners in a Rothstein-backed casino, following Arnold's suggestion that he see the booze-and-boodle-loaded hapless hooligan home.

So if Rothstein really was behind the 300 Club, Mrs. Willebrandt may have had second thoughts about ordering Maurice Campbell to destroy a joint presided over by so formidable an adversary. Among the otherwise unknown part-owners of Helen Morgan's place, no underworld name has come to light, so perhaps it was less risky to have Campbell and his underpaid agents tear up and plunder the chic Chez Morgan.

More likely, however, it was—as Stanley Walker concluded —Miss Morgan herself whom Mabel Walker Willebrandt wished literally to destroy. If this was true, the motive must have been largely personal—the jealous dislike of a thirty-eight-year-old, plain-faced former schoolteacher for a glamorous, gifted, extremely beautiful woman who had made it to the top, after seven disappointing years of failure and drudgery, as an artist for whom the definition "torch singer" was created—and, finally, as a nationally celebrated sensation in Florenz Ziegfeld's greatest Broadway production.

On the other hand (setting aside the personal element), the "wily and inscrutable" Willebrandt may simply have realized that a consistent persecution of Helen Morgan would bring her Prohibition department bigger and better headlines than she could achieve by any other device of harassment. At any rate, and for whatever complex reason, Mabel *was* out to get Helen, and her campaign toward that obsessive objective was already under way in the winter of 1928.

In early March the unlawfully confiscated Chez Morgan furnishings and fixtures were unloaded from warehouse trucks at 134 West 52nd Street, where, on a gala opening night, crowds of exuberant patrons surged through the basement door of a fine old brownstone into Helen Morgan's Summer Home.

There, in an atmosphere of soft lights and muted music, the customers dined, drank, and awaited the moment after midnight when the lights dimmed to rise again on the dark-haired, great-eyed woman in a simple Valentina gown, perched atop the Steinway with a long scarlet kerchief held in her white hands.

Morgan was back where she belonged, and all the attentive people sat in spellbound silence while she wove her elusive spell.

Helen appeared for a few weeks after the new club's opening, between 1 and 3 A.M. on week nights only. With this schedule she could spend her Sundays as she pleased, and she and Lulu sometimes went to call on Major Edward Bowles and his actress wife, Margaret Illington, in their lush penthouse atop the Capitol Theater building.

There the Bowleses and assembled guests could view, through a plate glass wall and over the theater balconies, the silent screen's weekly offering, and it was on one of these evenings that Helen met and charmed London's internationally known interior decorator, Lady Mendl.

The two girls fell to discussing design and period, and suddenly Elsie Mendl said, "Miss Morgan, you certainly know a lot more about this craft than I'd expect of a famous musical comedy star. Why, you speak of the Louis periods in the way a seasoned decorator does."

Miss Morgan murmured her thanks, and that was the start of a new hobby that would occupy her free hours for months and years to come.

A few days after Lady Mendl's commendation, a salesman in Gimbels' antique department, astonished to find La Morgan moving some Louis XIV chairs from a Louis XVI setting to their proper milieu, received the demure explanation, "Just trying to help out, dear. I'm sure it must distress you when misguided customers get your periods all mixed up."

Soon the lady had begun to consider herself a decorating authority and she felt it her bounden duty to advise all her friends regarding draperies, rugs, and the rearrangement of furniture.

Helen needed hobbies, since apparently here was no important man in her life at this time. Accordingly, in addition to haunting decorators' salons and Third Avenue antique shops, she passed some pleasant hours with Lulu cutting, stitching, and sewing, for a collection of dolls representing stage and screen charmers, costumes appropriate to the seasonal roles in which these ladies appeared.

Often the two women worked and gossiped well into the early morning hours. And on these occasions Helen rarely drank more than a single brandy and soda, while Lulu, who seldom felt the urge for alcohol, sipped at a glass of Moxie— an innocuous soft drink to which she'd been addicted since her girlhood.

In these days, Morgan drank sparsely in her leisure time, and seldom exceeded a reasonable quota during working hours.

This was altogether a tranquil interim for her, and soon, as proprietor Nicholas Blair was forced to turn away an overflow of patrons at the club's iron-grilled door, Arthur Benton saw to it that his client's salary jumped from $750 to $1,000 a week.

Then, when Blair persuaded her to appear on Sunday nights, she signed a new contract at $1,250 a week. Morgan was now giving eight performances in *Show Boat*, plus fourteen at the club each week, and the strain of such a strenuous schedule was bound to catch up with her.

Lately, the Summer Home had become an "in" place to be seen. All seemed to be going well there throughout the spring and Helen, gradually feeling secure as she continued to be surrounded by friendly, admiring faces, failed to detect chicanery when she was asked one night in June to join a party of three admirers.

As she followed the maître d' to the table, she noted that the men who rose to greet her wore their tailored tuxedos with ease and that their smiling woman companion's evening gown couldn't have come off a rack.

The taller man, John J. Mitchell, introduced his friends as Mr. and Mrs. Lon H. Tyson of Dallas, Texas.

Helen accepted the Tysons' gushing compliments with self-deprecating murmurs and sat down to make small talk, privately noting a quart of champagne in its silver bucket.

After a time she left the table, giving no more thought to the trio than to any other apparently affluent out-of-towners with whom she was asked to mingle.

The Tysons and Mitchell began to drop in regularly at the club and the men, who averaged a waiter's tip of $7.50, also usually gave the maître d' $10.00. This was par for the course for average well-to-do customers, and also these people professed to be ardent fans, so Helen became casually friendly with them.

Then, in the early hours of June 24 (a date she would soon have reason to remember), she sat down with these always amiable people who had been drinking whiskey.

Tyson asked if she'd like some champagne, and she answered, shrugging, "Oh, no, don't change over just for me."

Tyson said, "Then what about some brandy?"

Morgan told him, "Yes, do order brandy. I've been drinking it all evening. I *love* brandy." So Tyson summoned the waiter, who went away and came back, saying, "I'm sorry, sir, but we seem to be out of brandy."

Helen gave the waiter her slow, sweet smile. She said, "Tell Herman to come over here." Herman Brooks, her favorite waiter, came, and she asked him to go to her house and get six quarts of brandy, adding, "Tell Mama not to give you that Napoleon, but the other brandy."

Brooks left the club, aware that Miss M was a little tight,

since neither he nor Lulu Morgan had to be told that her Napoleon was not for public consumption.

After some of the brandy Herman brought in had been served to the festive foursome, Mrs. Tyson suddenly looked around the big room, musing. She said, "You know, I'd like to open a place like this in Dallas."

Helen looked at her woozily. "Then why don't you do as I do? There isn't any risk. Get a couple or three good fellows to go in with you. Then if there's any trouble, you're just an employee. They'll take the blame."

While she was at the table, Tyson bought two quarts of brandy at fifteen dollars each, but Helen apparently made no further reference to the club's operation, so she may have suddenly suspected, even through a haze of Three-Star Hennessy, that these people were not to be trusted. But then again, maybe not, for the revised methods recently employed by Mabel Willebrandt in her new enforcement campaign had become increasingly subtle.

John Mitchell, Lon Tyson, and Tyson's pretty wife had by this time endeared themselves to the club's employees as free-spenders and tippers; also, they bore no likeness whatever to the old-time easily recognized dry agents, so why should Helen or her "good fellows" suspect that their frequent visits to the club had been part of a plan of entrapment that would be concluded on this night of June 24, 1928?

This time Mabel Walker Willebrandt was out to make monster headlines. The stage was now set for her grandstand play in Mayor Walker's town, where, she was convinced, a national nucleus of wetness and underworld evil had evolved through Tammany Hall and Governor Alfred E. Smith, who hoped to run in the presidential race as Democratic candidate opposite the Republican party's ultra-conservative dry candidate, Herbert Hoover.

When Mabel had called on Walker to "pull together" with her, the tactful Jimmy, instead of reminding her that Washington was by her own admission no legalized Sahara, merely retaliated with certain facts.

He said that the New York Police had to enforce each day

"some 2,500 sections of the penal code, numerous city ordinances and traffic regulations," yet, even so, a single Broadway precinct had, since his election, turned in reports of 1,593 Volstead Act complaints to the Department of Justice—where "most of the cases" had been allowed to "die."

This was the kind of man Mabel had to deal with in Mayor Walker. But Jimmy was not so much to be despised as Smith, the Happy Warrior. There was a four-count villain as ever was: a Democrat, a Roman Catholic, a politician who'd publicly advocated certain revisions in the Volstead Act, and (last but by no means least) a self-educated roughneck who'd dared to refer to Mabel Willebrandt as "that Prohibition Portia."

Seething with righteous resentment against the mayor, the governor, Guinan, and Morgan, Mabel was now ready, in the final days of June, to assemble all her forces for an unprecedented attack upon Gomorrah on the Hudson.

The date was dramatically set for the night when cheering thousands in Houston, Texas, turned out to nominate Al Smith as the Democratic presidential candidate. And starting precisely at midnight on Thursday, June 28, some 160-odd federal agents, supervised by Major Campbell and one Shannon Thomas, closed eleven Manhattan nightclubs east and west between Fortieth and Fifty-third streets.

Most of the raiders were young, and all of them wore evening clothes. Working in squads of five or six, they visited (among less prominent places) Helen Morgan's Summer Home, the Jungle, Furnace, European, Mimic, Charm, Beaux Arts, Frivolity, Salon Royal, and Silver Slipper clubs.

In each place the young buckaroos made merry until the end of the first show, around 2 or 2:30 A.M., at which time a single squad member, having obtained "sufficient evidence," strode onto the dance floor, introduced himself as a federal agent, and ordered the club to be closed.

After that two or more squad members urged screaming customers onto the streets and herded club managers and their employees into patrol wagons, leaving their pals to pursue a search of the clubs' cleared premises for further evidence.

Oddly enough—since the papers observed that "no inkling of the Campbell raids had reached" the various clubs—the Misses Morgan and Guinan were not around when the stripling agents in evening attire padlocked their establishments. Worthy of note also was the odd behavior of a key squad member at Texas's sucker spot, which seemed to baffle a *New York Times* reporter.

This one entered the Salon Royal alone, purchased a bottle of champagne "to go," took it out to the sidewalk, unwrapped it, then reentered the club at the head of his coterie, evidence in hand.

Just what the young man expected to gain by this performance remains unclear, but then, who knows what curious notion of caution may have entered the mind of a new enforcement agent ordered to close a club operated by Larry Fay, which may also have been protected by Arnold Rothstein and his assistant bodyguard–hit man, Legs Diamond?

According to the *Times*, "wild scenes" ensued in every club just after a federal spokesman stepped out onto the dance floor. Singers, chorines, waiters, bus boys, musicians, and throngs of frantic patrons, many of whom had imbibed too freely while toasting the Happy Warrior, fled through the streets, East Side, West Side, and all around the midtown area of old Manhattan.

In a day or so Mrs. Willebrandt would deny that politics had anything to do with what a *Times* reporter described as "the largest series of raids on night clubs in New York since the passage of the National Prohibition Act."

If this was true, it does seem a pity that Mabel had staged her big show on June 28 when she was unable either to feel elated at having spoiled the fun of several thousand Smith fans or a sense of disappointment in not having nabbed those prime-time absentee entertainers, the Misses Morgan and Guinan.

As to the ladies' absence from their bailiwicks on this Thursday night of Major Campbell's "spectacular activity" one Guinan girl observed that this was the one raid occasion on which the Queen hadn't been present to bid the orchestra strike up "The Prisoner's Song" as she and her herd of G-stringed ponies trotted gaily out to the wagon.

One could understand why Miss Morgan, who had no liking for scandalous headlines, much less temporary imprisonment, would have fled her Summer Home at the least whispered warning that Campbell was coming, but not Miss Guinan who, ever alert for business-building publicity, had always welcomed encounters with the cornball federal agents and local coppers.

The question remains, then, if indeed their clubs' *managers* had no "inkling" of the Willebrandt invasion, how could these ladies have possibly got the message?

Whether or not they did remains uncertain, but one thing was sure: Somehow, overnight, they did get word that Campbell had threatened to issue warrants for their arrest if they failed to "surrender to the proper authorities," so the two most-wanted hostesses decided to give themselves up voluntarily on Friday, June 29.

That morning Helen rose early (for her) and went out to the kitchen where her mother, in a neat housedress and frilly apron, was fixing her breakfast of grapefruit, eggs, bacon, coffee, and buttered toast. And while Helen was putting away this hearty repast, Lulu reassured her that attorney J. Arthur Adler would be more than a match for Campbell today, as he had been in the past.

After a leisurely cigarette, Helen bathed, applied a touch of lipstick and eye shadow, dressed simply, and left the apartment to signal a taxi on Fifty-fourth Street.

Downtown, in her Greenwich Village apartment that was cluttered with long-legged dolls, garish bric-a-brac, and lacy pillows, Texas Guinan eased out of bed and began an elaborate daily ritual. Texas was forty-four and under no delusion as to the time and skill it took to paint on the hopefully deceptive, vivid mask with which she faced the day. She dressed herself to the nines, tilted a floppy, big-flowered hat over one mascaraed eye, and clomped downstairs onto Eighth Street. The house she lived in stood next to Alice Foote Macdougal's downtown restaurant, and today, Texas probably dropped in there for brunch.

Alice served marvelous food, and besides, the two women were friends, so they must have joked and chatted while scanning the *Times*' ironic account of Campbell's "spectacular activity." Then Texas left the restaurant and, greeting friends along the way, walked half a block to Sixth Avenue to flag a cab.

Downtown at the Federal Building she and Helen met and went together to Prohibition headquarters, prepared to give themselves up on "new charges of violating the Volstead Act."

They had, of course, expected to surrender to Maurice Campbell, but the first man they spoke to surprisingly said the major wasn't in. He then consulted with several other employees as to the boss's whereabouts, but nobody knew anything.

By this time Texas and Helen were somewhat bewildered. And after a thorough search of the headquarters offices had failed to reveal any documents whatsoever concerned with affidavits, accusations, or warranty charges, the two docile applicants for arrest asked what, exactly, they were supposed to do next.

One man said, "Well, I think you'd better go talk with U. S. Attorney Tuttle. Maybe he can find something you ladies can be accused of."

Both the ladies' eyebrows ascended. They had read Tuttle's adamant statement in the *Times*: "I will institute proceedings against ticket speculators and bail bond clerks, but never will I be the first server in a Prohibition prosecution." Consequently, on reaching Tuttle's office, they were not surprised to learn that he, too, had absented himself, leaving no word as to where he might be located.

They were received by Assistant U.S. Attorney Watts, who asked them, when they had stated their business, to be seated while he did some investigating. But even though Watts "scurried about" for sixty-nine minutes seeking some means of upholding the Volstead Act, he could find no papers drawn up against Morgan and Guinan.

Finally, through some legerdemain that the *Times* failed to make clear, the two suppliants, "having become defendants at last through proper channels," appeared at 1:00 P.M. before a U.S. commissioner named Cotter who told them, "You are charged with violating the national Prohibition law and will be held in $1,000 bail for further hearing July 19."

This disposition of the Morgan-Guinan contretemps must have been delivered in tired tones, for Cotter had already droned it ad nauseam. Before this long day ended, he would voice the same sentence 102 times in disposing of as many victims of the Willebrandt-Campbell raids.

Meanwhile, the outraged attorney J. Arthur Adler had been on hand to spit out an answer to reporters who asked why Miss Morgan had been made a defendant.

"Publicity," hissed Adler. "Venom is the explanation for Major Campbell's motive in this action."

Once again Adler was busy, as was Texas Guinan's lawyer, posting bail, and this time the situation seemed altogether absurd. Since neither Texas nor Helen had been present during the raids, the only grounds for arrest could be that they were principals in the operation of their clubs. Here was a rap that both women had successfully beat before, insisting that they were only salaried entertainers, and this was definitely true in Morgan's case.

The girls probably shared a taxi as far as Eighth Street, and though they could not have shared a convivial drink because Guinan was a teetotaler, the trip uptown must have been hilarious.

Texas may have stopped in again at Alice Foote Macdougal's to regale her with the day's events over a cup of coffee, and no stretch of the imagination is necessary to visualize Helen entering her apartment, calling out, "Mama, break out the Napoleon. It's been one hell of a crazy day, but Adler says it's all gonna be all right."

Whether or not it was really going to be all right remained to be seen. Hearing that Adler had accused him of being a publicity-seeker with venomous motives, Campbell told reporters, "I did not order the arrest of Miss Morgan and Miss

Guinan. These two young women went to the Federal Building voluntarily and such action as was taken against them was not through me. I am not responsible for what the attorney for either may say about me."

Reading this, one is left to wonder who could have erred in warning the women that Campbell meant to arrest them if they failed to give themselves up voluntarily—and if indeed the good major had no such intention, then the pair had certainly put themselves through a wholly unnecessary, not to say senseless, ordeal.

Throughout the month of July Helen enjoyed a respite from the Summer Home's late hours. During this period she must have spent considerable time conferring with Adler, and certainly he assured her that everything would go well.

By his own admission U.S. Attorney Charles S. Tuttle had no wish to be involved in the forthcoming trials. His long and arduous negotiations with Adler in an effort to straighten out the deplorable situation Campbell had created by illegally wrecking Chez Morgan had resulted in Helen's finally (and generously) agreeing not to press charges against the Prohibition authorities, once Tuttle had effected her exoneration and ordered the return of the club's furnishings.

Plainly Tuttle had far more respect for Morgan and Adler than he had for either Campbell or Mabel Willebrandt, and he must have felt truly confident as to the outcome of his client's latest, most ludicrous brush with the law.

If that was the case, then Adler was surely flabbergasted by the court proceedings that transpired at the end of the month.

On July 31 the *New York Times* carried this headline: "Texas Guinan and Helen Morgan Indicted in War on the Night Clubs."

In court on the previous day Federal Judge Frank T. Coleman had accepted eighteen true bills that mentioned eighteen nightclubs. One hundred and eight persons alleged to "have some part" in the club's operations were indicted by the federal grand jury for "conspiracy"—and the names of Morgan and Guinan led all the rest.

Furthermore, Assistant U.S. Attorney Watts, head of the Prohibition division of Tuttle's office, who (along with another attorney named Arthur Schwartz) offered up grand jury evidence, frankly stated that he intended to use "all the teeth in the law."

Until this time "conspiracy" charges had been limited to distillery operations, liquor warehouse thefts, rum running, and "rum ring" gangsters. Now a conspiracy violation of the Prohibition law included "the illegal operation of a night club, even a speakeasy, with the aid of others who may be merely employees." The 102 indictments also charged "the maintenance of a nuisance," with a maximum penalty of a year's jail sentence and a thousand-dollar fine.

Even a fool could see that Mabel Walker Willebrandt was still determined to put Miss Helen Morgan out of business.

In La Guinan she had a hard nut to crack because (as previously stated) the Queen's repeated arrests, convictions, and releases, not to mention her outspoken contempt for all Prohibition enforcement methods, had made her a consistently less newsworthy, not to say embarrassing adversary.

Wisely and shrewdly now, having trumped up a reason for arresting and arraigning the most glamorous entertainer in the night world of New York, Mabel Willebrandt sat back in her swivel chair and relaxed, awaiting the result of her own and Campbell's latest act of unjustified persecution.

Those results were not long in coming. Around the first of August Helen Morgan, no longer reassured by Adler's optimism, succumbed to panic, went straight as a homing pigeon to Ziegfeld's private office, and sobbed, "Flo, you've got to help me. I can't take this any more."

Ziegfeld was ready and willing to help her, for though he'd decreed that no one should be starred in *Show Boat*, the public had already acclaimed Helen Morgan as the production's first-magnitude luminary.

At the show's tryout opening night in Washington Ziegfeld

had realized the effect that Morgan and "Bill" would always have on an audience. He knew, as did Kern and Hammerstein, that this Julie Dozier was, quite simply, irreplaceable. Besides, Ziggy had grown extremely fond of Helen, and he'd been concerned, since the first of the year, about the effect that late hours at the Summer Home, plus heavy drinking and federal harassment, might have on this sensitive, deeply emotional woman.

Morgan was a priceless theater property, but more than that she was somebody Flo Ziegfeld cared about as a human being. Unlike other close-fisted, cold-blooded New York producers, this gentleman paid his people big salaries and took a sincere interest in their personal lives.

Mr. Z had already become, to such stars as Fannie Brice and Will Rogers, not only the Great Showman but a friend on whom they could depend—a man, indeed, whose indiscriminate concern for principals, chorus girls, and crew members of his various *Follies* productions had caused one wag to dub him the Great White Father.

All this is true about Ziegfeld, and if the above paragraph sounds like saccharine sentimentality, let the skeptical reader think what he pleases. The truth is that Florenz Ziegfeld, like Helen Morgan, was not only weirdly extravagant but almost unbelievably generous. Mr. Z had faults, such as extramarital attachments to at least three theatrical beauties, and a limited sense of humor that caused him to look upon certain comedians as rather tiresome buffoons the public demanded along with his glorified girls in the *Follies*, but the positive, indisputable fact remains that nobody who worked for this man ever had reason to nurture a lasting grudge against him.

And so, for business and personal reasons, Flo Ziegfeld was now determined to stand behind Helen Morgan at a time when she needed his sympathetic guidance.

The *New York Times* of August 6 carried a story headlined, "Miss Morgan Ends Nightclub Career," which opened with the following sentence.

Her difficulties encountered in connection with the Prohibition law have driven Helen Morgan, musical comedy star,
out of night club entertaining, the Ziegfeld office announced
yesterday.

The two-column piece, which cited Campbell's destructive
Christmas raid and Helen's agreement not to bring charges
against the national Prohibition people, also contained this
observation: "That she was unhappy in the role of defendant
was quite obvious."

The *Times* story continued: "Her recent indictment was
apparently the last straw which determined her to cut loose
from any environment where she might find herself face to
face with a Prohibition agent." Going on to say that even
though Miss Morgan had always insisted she was employed
at both Chez Morgan and her Summer Home only as a paid
entertainer, she would now "refuse to be bound by any contract that threw her so persistently into hot water."

Finally, Ziegfeld was directly quoted as saying, "Miss Morgan has ended the cabaret chapter of her career. She will now
conserve all her energies for her work as a featured artist of
the legitimate stage. She has taken a house in Great Neck and
given up late hours and overwork."

Soon the statement that she had given up cabaret work
would prove to have been premature. Within a year, actually,
she would be working in cabaret at the New Amsterdam
Roof for Ziegfeld himself, and after four years she would
return, with Repeal, to an outstanding Manhattan nightclub.

In line with this circumstance, it is interesting to note that
two men indicted along with her and other nightclub people
after the June raids were listed as part-owners and managers
of the European Club at 26 West 53rd Street.

These men were Greeks and their names—Nick Prounis
and Peter Kledauris—leap out from a page in the *Times* as
significant in the story of Helen Morgan, for they would bring
her back, in the fall of 1933, to triple business at their club.

On Tuesday, August 7, the Federal Building courtroom

where the dry war session got under way was packed with sensation seekers. More than a third of the 130 persons indicted on nuisance charges failed to appear, but Texas Guinan made her entrance in flowered crepe de Chine, booming, "Is this an invitational affair?" Then she further delighted her fans by describing the court procedure as "a lot of bologna."

In regard to Helen Morgan, Tex had already told the press, "As usual, they got the wrong party. She's just a dumb, twenty-three-year-old kid."

Guinan certainly knew that Helen, at twenty-seven, was no dumb kid, so she must have made the statement hoping to build up Morgan's public image of a post-adolescent, dreamily unaware of underworld contacts, even though one or more gangsters may have been secretly backing Nick Blair, who'd managed both Chez Morgan and the Summer Home.

This may have been partly true, since Helen was, by nature, amiably aloof and therefore on intimate terms with no more than a few people. She was neither "dumb" nor stupid, but she was not (like Texas) tough-minded, mercenary, nor addicted to ribald wisecracks.

Texas was frankly out to give an impression of a hardboiled, realistic broad with no illusions regarding a racket controlled by mobsters and plagued by hypocritical, often crooked, federal agents.

Helen, on the other hand, had somehow managed, all through her club career, to present a picture of woozy naïveté behind a sphinxlike facade that really concealed a conviction that general reticence in a songbird who knew when *not* to sing was a trait that would be appreciated in underworld social circles.

On August 7 she was not in court when ninety-odd persons pleaded guilty to charges of maintaining a nuisance, but attorney Adler promised she would appear the next day, albeit not to plead guilty to any charge.

On Wednesday, when she did appear, Adler told the judge that he'd fight the charges brought against his innocent client, and if (as one reporter observed) she "looked as though she'd rather be any place else than where she was," she gave no sign of the kind of tension a fearful guilty party might betray.

When she had faced the judge with dignified demeanor, she left the Federal Building and returned to her apartment, where Lulu was sorting out things to be packed for the move to Long Island.

6

Helen Morgan on Trial

THE HOUSE THAT HELEN had rented in Great Neck stood next to the home of celebrity-loving Frank Case, owner and manager of New York's Algonquin Hotel, which teemed from lobby to roof with showpeople, novelists, and newspaper columnists.

Frank and his amiable wife proved to be delightful neighbors. Their daughter, Margaret, was a talented, witty girl, and their small son, Carroll, who was at the tricycle age, frequently had to be summoned at mealtimes from Lulu Morgan's fragrant kitchen, where he'd sat munching warm cookies and gazing big-eyed at Helen, whom he'd decided to marry as soon as he grew up.

In 1928 the tree-shaded town of Great Neck had become a chic suburban retreat for all kinds of theatrical performers, musicians, and writers. It was a fine place for any show biz person to live in, and both the Morgans enjoyed this actual summer home of Helen's, "just forty-five minutes from Broadway" and the padlocked brownstone that now seemed haunted by specters of *agents provocateurs* posing as paying guests.

After midnight at the so-called Summer Home, Helen had worked a graveyard shift ending in the small hours that might soon have led to a killing routine of too much brandy, sleeping pills, and daytime capsule stimulants. But this would not have been solely the outcome of either overwork or the Willebrandt-Campbell campaign, for Helen Morgan had become deeply involved in a frustrating love-sex alliance that had lately become an obsession.

Since her association with Philip Charig, who'd written "Nobody Wants Me" for her in *Americana,* Morgan had been, aside from her crush on Oscar Hammerstein, romantically interested in one man only.

This glamorous woman, who was both religious and conventional, loathed promiscuity and desperately yearned to be married. She had always lived at home with Lulu, and whether sober or soused, she could never be lured into a one-night stand situation.

Actually, for a girl who'd grown up in show business, Morgan was astonishingly square in her attitude toward sexual congress. She enjoyed the company of clever gay boys such as Francis X. (Rubber Face) Mahoney, and because she was incapable of deliberate cruelty, she managed to conceal an aversion to lesbianism. She had few close friends among women, and one old friend of hers has stated emphatically, "I think she'd have fainted dead away if either a femme or a dyke had ever made a pass at her."

Actor George Blackwood, who was once Helen's lover, recalls that she was almost childlike in bed, and that even the few mild deviations she allowed herself from so-called "normal intercourse" sometimes troubled her conscience.

Yearning always toward a lasting legal alliance, Morgan had no desire (perhaps because of her mother's lone struggle to bear her and bring her up) to bear any man's children.

She just wanted to marry a man she loved, and for some time now she had known a tycoon who bore no resemblance to the "ordinary" man she sang about in *Show Boat.* Here was a fellow who was handsome, rich, personable, and influential. He was also deeply attached to Helen, but there was one unalterable stumbling block to the realization of a near-ideal union: This paragon, already married, either could not or would not divorce his wife.

Down the years Helen would sing, with transparent, heart-wrenching poignancy, a song that ran, "The one I love belongs to somebody else," and that was how it would be for her with this man as long as she lived.

He was Arthur Loew, and his father was Marcus Loew of the Loew Theater Enterprises. Born October 5, 1897, Arthur was three years older than Helen. After graduating from New York University, he'd worked for a time as a cub reporter on the New York *Evening Graphic*; then, after the Loews had taken over the Metro Pictures Corporation in 1920, Arthur went to work for his father, becoming in 1927 first vice president of Loew's Incorporated, which controlled Metro Goldwyn Mayer.

He belonged to various clubs in New York and on Long Island, where he lived in a beautiful house. Gossip along the Rialto had it that because his wife was in a sanitarium he could not divorce her in order to marry Broadway's most beautiful ex-nightclub hostess, who also was the star of *Show Boat*, but no one was absolutely sure about that. All that can be said is that Arthur Loew was the *one, one man in the world* for Helen Morgan. More than all her troubles with the Prohibition authorities, this secret, illegal alliance was haunting her, night and day. The daughter of Lulu Morgan, a prim farm girl who'd also loved one man alone, hadn't been raised to live "in sin" without being plagued by a rigorous Christian conscience.

Nevertheless, this was a one-man woman who'd finally found her man, and no amount of guilt feelings could force Helen Morgan to let him go. Suffering, she clung to the hope that a day would come when Loew's home situation would change and he'd be able to make her an honest woman.

Until that day she would love and suffer in silence, except in the moments when she climbed up on a piano to pour forth her heart's intolerable longings in "My Bill" and "Can't Help Lovin' That Man"—two songs she could sing like nobody else.

At some time in the autumn of 1928 Morgan recorded these songs and posed for a silhouette to be used in the pro-

logue of a part-talkie Hollywood film version of *Show Boat*.
And since she was not overworked that fall, she passed a
pleasant Christmas and New Year's with Lulu, the Case family, and various show business friends who also lived in Great
Neck.

In January 1929, when a flu epidemic swept Manhattan,
Helen was stricken on Thursday, January 10, but she stayed
with the show through the next Monday night's performance.

On Tuesday she was too ill to get out of bed and Lulu called
an ambulance to whisk her off to a private sanitarium. Her
understudy, Eunice Tierney, went on for three nights and one
matinée, but the doughty original Julie Dozier was back on
top of the piano on the night of Friday, January 18.

Although Helen was fond of Miss Tierney, this was the first
time that frustrated young woman had been able to show what
she could do with Julie. In spite of raids, arrests, court appearances, and occasional bouts with brandy, Miss Morgan had
never failed to be in the wings before the rise of *Show Boat*'s
curtain. It had taken a plague to lay her prone, and even so
her superb recuperative powers, plus a fanatical devotion to
this one great role of her life, had brought her back, triumphant over chills and fever, after three days and three nights
in bed.

Beyond this illness, nothing of significance happened to her
until the morning of April 8—a bluc Monday the *Times*
called "Night Club Day"—which found her in federal court
for the calendar reading, but Judge Edwin S. Thomas of
Connecticut was too busy imposing fines and sentences on
other raid victims to reach the cases of Morgan and Guinan
before five o'clock.

Texas, who'd been told the judge wouldn't get around to
her on Monday, had stayed at home, but Thomas advised
Arthur Adler to return with his chic client the following morning. She was on her way out of the building when the boys
from the papers surrounded her, asking, "Miss Morgan, what
do you think of the Jones law?"

She gave them her beautiful smile as she asked with big-eyed innocence, "What is the Jones law?" Then, as she walked with the ring of scribes toward the courtroom doors, she reminded them all that she was out of the nightclub business.

If Helen had been reading the papers, she certainly knew all about this Jones Act—the latest, toughest Prohibition law, which imposed a maximum five-year jail sentence and a ten-thousand-dollar fine on bootleggers for even a first offense. However, by this time she probably felt that she need never concern herself again with the fate of bootleggers nor anyone else involved with speakeasy operations.

Her concern for herself was another thing, and she was somewhat encouraged when, within a few days, Texas Guinan was acquitted of the charge of maintaining a nuisance.

On April 14 Arthur Adler told the press, "My client is ready for trial and we will fight the nuisance charge." After the recent collapse of previous cases on the "conspiracy" charge, Adler knew there was no chance of his client's facing that accusation. Her defense would therefore be the same as before in regard to Chez Morgan: even though this defunct club had been called Helen Morgan's Summer Home, she'd had no part, as a salaried entertainer, in the business of running the place.

Adler assured the press that records and papers seized during the last federal raid would prove that his client had always received a regular weekly salary. He said that he hadn't as yet been able to get his hands on those papers, but still had hopes of doing so. Even if he did not, however, Miss Morgan's contract and checkbook would establish her status as a paid employee only.

On Wednesday, April 17, the Morgan case went to trial after considerable delay in assembling a jury of twelve men ranging from late middle age to nigh senility. Four of these were retirees, two had no occupations, and one (surely included because the lawyers were scraping the barrel's bottom) admitted that he was against the enforcement methods employed by Mabel Willebrandt and Major Campbell.

In his opening address U.S. Attorney Leslie Salter of Willebrandt's staff encountered a bumptious adversary in attorney

Adler. Salter had barely managed to inform the jury that Miss Morgan and nine men were charged with maintaining a nuisance at the Summer Home when Adler's glib objections brought the prosecutor's opening speech to a close.

The government's first witness was John J. Mitchell, lately revealed as one of a quartet of federal agents whom their colleagues called the Four Horsemen.

Mitchell told of repeated visits to the Summer Home, usually with both of the Tysons, before the early morning hour of June 24 when Miss Morgan, after sending Brooks, the waiter, over to her house for brandy, had told Mrs. Tyson, who'd said she wanted to open a nightclub in Dallas, that she should get "a couple or three good fellows" to go in with her and take the blame in case of trouble.

He also told (only he and God knew why) of a night when Miss Morgan had sat on the bar of the Furnace Club, singing "Ol' Man River" and tossing dollar bills to the Negro musicians.

When Adler asked Mitchell, in cross-examination, why, when he'd witnessed certain law violations at the Summer Home, he hadn't made a few arrests, the witness answered, "Because I was trying to get the higher-ups."

Adler then moved in, wagging a rapid forefinger. "Now, Mr. Mitchell, admit it. Didn't you make up that statement about Miss Morgan's arrangement to be considered as an employee?"

Mitchell immediately reared up, shouting, "Don't point your finger at me, please. *No.* That is absolutely true."

When he stepped down from the stand, Lou Tyson took his place to repeat in essential detail the story his predecessor had told, and after this testimony Judge Thomas ruled that court would adjourn until the next day.

The morning session on April 18 opened with a further cross-examination of Tyson, but Adler had fired only two questions when Judge Thomas, cupping his right ear, called him and Salter to the bench and told them, "I can't hear a thing."

His Honor declared a recess, retired to his chambers for

half an hour, then returned to the bench and almost immediately ordered an adjournment until 2 P.M.

Back in his chambers again Thomas told reporters that he'd been bothered lately by a "ringing" in his left ear. Yesterday, a louder ringing in his right ear had prevented his hearing many of the lawyers' questions and the dry agent's replies, and he feared that this condition might be the aftermath of a "minor intestinal operation."

During this recess Thomas visited a doctor who decided his condition might be due to overwork, and when he returned to the bench at two o'clock the judge declared that his hearing was somewhat improved.

Now, however, the proceedings directly related to Morgan were halted again while Nicholas Blair, the Summer Home's former manager, was brought before the bench. Because of his failure to appear the day before as Helen's chief co-defendant, Blair's bail of a thousand dollars had been forfeited, and Thomas had ordered a bench warrant for his arrest.

On the ground that Blair had been guilty of "willful default" in an effort to "embarrass" the U.S. government, Leslie Salter asked that new bail be set at five thousand dollars, and also that Blair be forced under oath to answer charges made by the government.

Thomas gave an order to that effect, and granted a motion by Blair's attorney, Lewis Koenig, to reduce the new bail from five to one thousand dollars, when Koenig explained that Blair had thought the trial would be postponed because of a death in Arthur Adler's family.

Throughout all these proceedings the jury had been out of the box. Now the twelve were recalled to hear Blair, as Helen's chief co-defendant, offer a surprising plea of guilty. Six other co-defendants had pleaded guilty; a bench warrant had been issued for the arrest of the absent Herman Brooks; and now, as one reporter wryly observed, Miss Morgan, who was pleading not guilty, was "standing trial alone."

When Blair had made his plea, Salter once more held up the trial for fifteen minutes by requesting a hearing on the charge of "willful default."

Repeating himself, the prosecutor said, "I had understood Blair would plead guilty, yet, when the case is called, he ducks out to embarrass this trial. Your Honor fixed his bail at five thousand dollars yesterday. Perhaps that has something to do with his appearance here today. It is a practice in nightclub cases here for defendants to whip-saw the court and the government around to suit their own convenience."

Finally Tyson was recalled to the witness stand, where he repeated the story of Helen's "good fellows" and identified, as having been purchased by him and Mitchell at the Summer Home, six near-empty half-pint rye and brandy bottles and two quart bottles that had contained champagne.

Adler then got down to business and forced Tyson to admit new evidence: to wit, that his wife, who wasn't an accredited agent, had been paid, in twice-weekly Treasury Department checks, five dollars a day by Willebrandt's department.

When Adler reminded the witness that every dry agent was required to pass a civil service examination, Tyson said that his wife was a "special employee."

In answer to Adler's question, "To whom did your wife report?" Tyson said, "I reported for her and for myself."

Under intensive grilling Tyson revealed that he'd stayed first in New York at the Chesterfield and Presidential hotels, where he'd paid $3.50 a day for a room and $1.50 a day for food, thus using up the $5-a-day sustenance fund Mabel had granted him along with his regular salary. Then, before Tyson knew it, Adler had him admitting that when he'd moved to the Hotel McAlpin, the government, "for some unexplained reason," had paid for his room, leaving him his $5 a day to spend on food.

Asked if he and his fellow agents hadn't worked out "plans and schemes" for purchasing booze and garnering other evidence at the Summer Home, Tyson confessed that they had. But when Adler persisted, shouting, "Isn't it true that you people did, in fact, lay a trap to bring about Miss Morgan's arrest?" Tyson answered, "I wouldn't say it was a trap, though I may be wrong."

Exasperated, Adler now rapped out: "You testified your wife asked Miss Morgan's advice about opening a nightclub in Dallas, Texas. Isn't it clear in your mind that this question was propounded to trap Miss Morgan?"

Tyson said, "Yes, sir."

Adler then pressed his advantage, sneering, "Is it part of your Southern chivalry to introduce your wife to a lady for the purpose of trapping her?"

But this time U.S. Attorney Salter sprang up, warning that "no inference should be drawn against a public officer for doing his duty," and Judge Thomas decreed that Adler's last question be stricken from the record.

Adler now asked Tyson if he thought he was a gentleman. And when the witness answered, "Yes, sir," the attorney changed his tack to inquire, "You're a rye whiskey drinker, aren't you?"

"No," Tyson told him, "just for the purpose of getting a search warrant."

Adler, plainly weary, allowed Tyson to step down.

Mitchell was recalled to the stand and, after identifying the "evidence bottles," he confessed that at the time Helen was supposed to be drinking with his party, "hardly a drink" was left in the last bottle he and Tyson had ordered.

A chemist hired by Willebrandt was called upon to testify that he'd used about four ounces from each bottle in making his booze analysis, and Salter rose to announce that "aside from one or two more questions to one more witness," the government would rest its case.

As the court adjourned, the news hounds encircled Helen and her attorney. They asked whether or not she would take the stand, and Adler told them, "She certainly will. We have nothing to fear. We will have one or two more witnesses."

As he made this statement, Helen, who'd been "quiet and self-effacing" all through the tedious day, "smiled faintly."

Her behavior thus far, a *Times* writer noted, had been in "striking contrast to Texas Guinan who recently was acquitted of a similar charge."

He and all the other reporters who admired Helen for her composure would doubtless have been astounded had they been able to follow her home. Despite Arthur Adler's consistent assurance that she had nothing to fear, Helen was scared. Unlike Texas, who'd persuaded herself that the whole procedure was a senseless farce, Helen was living a nightmare and there is no doubt that when she reached her apartment this sensitive, essentially childlike woman broke down and wept in Lulu's arms.

As Morgan entered the courtroom the following morning, the hall buzzed with excitement. Well-groomed, smartly dressed, apparently composed, she sat through Salter's opening gambit in which he reiterated the dry agents' oft-repeated testimony anent the brandy Herman Brooks had brought from her house, the "impression" she'd given Mitchell and Tyson of being a partner of Nick Blair's, and the night at the Furnace Club when she'd made whoopee perched on the bar.

When the government decided to rest, Arthur Adler, to the crowd's utter astonishment, approached the bench with a motion that the case against his client be dismissed.

Judge Thomas denied the motion, and once again a gasp of surprise swept the courtroom as Adler called—not the beautiful star witness everyone had expected—but Arthur Benton, the lady's ex-manager.

On the stand Benton stated that during his thirty-year career as an actors' representative he'd managed, besides Helen Morgan, such luminaries as Laurette Taylor, Ina Claire, Irene Bordoni, Alice Brady, Mary Eaton, and W. C. Fields.

Benton said that he'd drawn up Miss Morgan's contract for *Show Boat*, and also every contract she'd made with Nicholas Blair. On his advice his client had signed with Blair (after refusing other nightclub offers) to appear at first between 1 and 3 A.M. on week nights only, at a salary of $750 a week. Later on, agreeing to work on Sundays, she'd signed another contract with Blair to be paid $1,000 a week, and later still a contract calling for $1,250 a week.

Under Salter's cross-examination Benton swore that Helen, as a paid entertainer at Chez Morgan and the Summer Home, had never "shared in the profits" of either place.

When Salter, with a strange irrelevance, asked if Benton hadn't once had some "little trouble" with Miss Morgan, Benton answered, "Yes, but not about contracts. All artists are that way, you know, and Miss Morgan is no different than the others."

In answer to Salter's question as to whether he'd gone sometimes to the Morgan clubs, Benton replied, "Yes, but I never bought liquor there because my visits were in the summer and I don't drink during the hot season." He smiled, and added impishly, "I do have liquor on my yacht, though."

Salter looked nonplused, then asked, "Didn't Miss Morgan once refuse to pay you ten percent of her salary, saying she'd drawn her latest contract with Blair herself and didn't owe you anything, and then didn't you write Blair for a copy of this contract?"

Benton sat up, plainly indignant, and snapped back, "She never said a word to me about my not being entitled to my commissions."

Before Salter was through, Benton revealed that, even though he'd known about the Chez Morgan's destructive raid, he'd advised Helen to sign again with Blair (surely implying that no one had expected the debacle on the Smith nomination night) inasmuch as the Summer Home was one of the most "exclusive" clubs in New York.

As Benton left the stand, Adler rose to say, "Your Honor, the defense rests," and "a murmur of surprise and disappointment came from the crowd."

All through Benton's testimony, the *Times* reporter had noticed Helen's "extreme nervousness" and the fact that "her hands shook and she seemed on the verge of tears."

In his summing up Adler accused the Prohibition authorities of using low entrapment methods and allowing dry agents to spend large sums of money in their entrapment program.

"Plainly," he said, "they were out to get someone of prominence, one whose name would appear on the front page."

Referring to the Mitchell-Tyson charade at the Summer Home on June 24, Adler cried, "They deliberately planned to entrap Miss Morgan. Can you imagine men stooping so low as to try to make you believe that Miss Morgan's mother was a bootlegger?"

Then, carried away perhaps by indignation (for it was true that Helen had talked too much on June 24) he shouted, "Can you, by the wildest stretch of the imagination, believe that Miss Morgan, who'd met these agents but a short time before, advised the wife of one of them to go into the nightclub business by getting three good fellows who, in case of trouble, would take the blame and say she was only an employee?"

Adler was not above using melodramatic tactics, and now he pulled out most of the stops. "Yet, for your money as taxpayers you get this kind of enforcement. You get men who shoot at women and fire on defenseless boats so they can justify themselves before certain hypocrites. A conviction in this case would be an approval of enforcement activities which have been condemned throughout the country."

When Adler had finished, he sat down beside his client and reached for her cold hand.

Helen smiled when he whispered something to her, but she still sat tense and fearful as the prosecuting attorney rose to begin his summing up.

Salter started out admitting, in regard to Mitchell's and Tyson's efforts to entrap Miss Morgan, "Of course the agents had to tell a lie, but the government approves of that." Then he continued, "Had the defense been able to get one witness who could truthfully deny the sale of liquor at the club, he would have been here and it would have been shouted from the house tops."

Suddenly sweeping his gaze over the audience and back past Helen to the jury, this incredible prosecutor said, "I compliment the defendant in this case. She has conducted herself like a lady in court. There has been no wisecracking around here."

Then, after the compliment, which was delivered in a mild tone, this U.S. government attorney cut loose with melodramatic, reasonless ranting worthy of a Bible Belt country lawyer circa 1890: "But this woman, with her God-given talent, has sold her birthright for a mess of pottage. She has betrayed her talents for $1,000 a week. [In Salter's excitement he'd forgotten the ante had risen in 1928 at the Summer Home to $1,250 a week.] Your duty is to the youth of our land, the young girls especially, who look at stars like Helen Morgan and say if she can play in a play like *Show Boat* and then make $1,000 a week in some nightclub, why can't they do likewise? By such conduct she would influence young girls to go slinking down the pathway to corruption and crime."

Finally ending his ungrammatical oratory, Salter walked toward his seat—and this writer can only regret that the *Times* man who quoted him word for word failed to record the effect this tirade had on the courtroom's occupants. Helen kept a straight face, so she must either have summoned enormous control or else have been temporarily so distrait as to be actually frightened by Salter's mock-revivalist nonsense.

Now, speaking for thirty minutes, Judge Thomas instructed the jury. He told them that, since by law any place where liquor was distilled or sold constituted a common nuisance, they must decide whether the Summer Home could be so classified.

"It is not necessary," Thomas told the jurors, "for you to establish that Miss Morgan was a proprietor, but only to satisfy yourselves beyond a reasonable doubt that she had aided, abetted, counseled, or assisted the proprietors in maintaining a nuisance, in order to justify a verdict of guilty."

As the jury filed out at 4:35 P.M. to deliberate, Helen Morgan suddenly burst into tears.

Before 7 P.M., when the jurors went out to supper, the ballot stood eight to four for acquittal. At 7 P.M. only one sanctimonious diehard was still holding out for a verdict of guilty.

Finally at 8:55 one juror knocked on the jury room door, signifying that a verdict had been reached.

Reporters noted that Helen Morgan sat "pale and trembling" while the twelve men filed into the box. As the foreman rose and gave the verdict: "Not guilty," the *Times* man thought, "she seemed about to faint," but somehow "gained control of herself." Then, crying softly at first, she "began to weep unrestrainedly."

Because few spectators could present the necessary credentials to reenter the Federal Building after its usual closing time, the courtroom was cleared without undue demonstration.

Judge Thomas, who'd cupped his hand to his troublesome right ear as the foreman spoke, seemed "puzzled by the verdict."

Prosecutor Salter seemed just "mildly surprised," but Arthur Adler, unmistakably pleased and proud, told the reporters: "I had expected this verdict and it is just."

As for Helen Morgan, after a visible effort at self-control, she said only, "I don't want to think any more about it."

During the past few days she had been on the verge of hysteria. No one had ever been able to quell her fearsome half-belief that she might be sentenced to at least one year in Manhattan's miserable prison for women. She was an intelligent person but also (as has been said) a naïve, insecure creature with a fatalistic attitude and the sometimes exaggerated fears of an overimaginative child.

This is not even surprising, since in possessing these personality traits Helen Morgan was not unique. Similar traits have been recognized by astute biographers in at least six ultra-glamorous stage and screen actresses who have died in the last three decades. Laurette Taylor, Jeanne Eagels, Tallulah Bankhead, Marilyn Monroe, Jean Harlow, and the ultra-sensitive Judy Garland were all child-women possessed of little-girl qualities, who needed constant, compassionate attention and understanding. All of them but one (Harlow) drank too much, or popped up-and-down pills, and died before their times.

Actually, Helen Morgan's common sense (and she did have some) must have told her that Adler was right in believing she'd emerge from this farcical trial a free woman, but there was always inside her the fatherless small girl who'd worked from the age of fourteen at menial jobs, gone hungry, and,

over seven long years, weathered far too many disappointments in the terrifying Broadway rat race.

Morgan was a mama's girl who, despite her indiscriminate
generosity, felt unable to number among her casual friends
more than a few whom she felt she could trust.

Always there would be Lulu. Just now there also were
Arthur Adler, Florenz Ziegfeld, and her lover, Arthur Loew,
but nobody else. These four people had helped her to get
through the trial, yet the whole experience had left her on
the verge of a nervous breakdown.

She would be a long time in recovering from the punishment inflicted upon her by Major Campbell and Mabel Willebrandt in a deliberate campaign to degrade, humiliate and—
if possible—imprison the star of *Show Boat*, who was also
Manhattan's outstanding nightclub attraction.

On the day after Helen's acquittal, Herman Brooks and the
other Summer Home waiters were fined and given suspended
sentences.

Nick Blair, who received a suspended six-month sentence
"on good behavior," was also fined three hundred dollars and
placed on probation for three years.

When the waiters were arraigned for sentence, Adler told
Judge Thomas, "Your Honor, these men are waiters, not
criminals. They have been supplying a demand because they
had to do so. New York's best people demand drinks with
their meals."

Leslie Salter immediately sprang up, shouting, "Although
I am not a New Yorker, I want to register an emphatic protest
against this defamatory statement. . . . New York's best people do not violate the law or induce others to violate it. These
nightclubs are patronized largely by out-of-town patrons. Certainly we cannot class the group that patronizes nightclubs
and violates the law as representing the best people anywhere."

Well, it is not hard to imagine the effect this outburst had
on the courtroom in 1929, when more than a thousand speakeasies and nightclubs in Manhattan were serving customers
ranging in social status from congressmen, governors, yachts-
men, and members of the Long Island horsey set, all the way

down to Willebrandt's free-spending but poorly paid Four Horsemen and their ilk.

By now nobody with real good sense had the slightest patience with Prohibition. Only the day before the *New York Times* had carried a front-page story in which the *Leviathan*'s new private owners had stated that, whereas the fabulous liner's recent crossing to Paris must be defined as "still officially dry, but unofficially wet, . . . this hypocritical state of affairs" would be changed on her return voyage. Passengers disembarking at Le Havre described the trip over as being "satisfactorily wet" due to an unloading of the ship's ample supply of medicinal alcohol, but one affluent New York buyer who'd crossed on the liner 201 times saw things differently. Observing that the price of drinks had dropped from seventy-five to fifty cents, Charles Kurzman decided that the ship's stewards, anticipating a "wet" return voyage, had unloaded their stock of booze at bargain prices.

In regard to the nation's prime exponent of blatant hypocrisy, the *Times* of April 19 carried a bulletin issued by Mabel Willebrandt in Washington. Declining to say what sort of future enforcement plans she had in mind, the lady declared that she was not really dissatisfied with the general results of the March 29 raids, arrests, and arraignments.

Ignoring the fact that more than a hundred people had been indicted, Mrs. Willebrandt was pleased to note that "about 65 persons had pled guilty, or been found so, whereas only two, the Misses Morgan and Guinan, had been acquitted."

Actually, by putting Helen out of the nightclub business, Willebrandt had gotten exactly nowhere in her foolhardy attempt to dry up Manhattan Island. Tammany Hall and Mayor James Walker were still going strong. Texas Guinan, in partnership with Larry Fay, would keep right on doing business at various stands, and within four years a new President—Franklin Delano Roosevelt—sick to death of the Prohibition travesty, would enforce Repeal, thereby putting big-time mobsters, bootleggers, crooked dry agents, and Assistant U.S. Attorney Mabel Walker Willebrandt out of business.

7

Applause *and* Sweet Adeline

ALL THROUGH THE EVENTFUL YEAR of 1929 Helen Morgan would have need of physical stamina, but most especially in the spring when she'd begin commuting to Astoria, Queens, to make a "talkie" at the lately reopened Eastern Paramount studio.

This situation had come about through an unprecedented upheaval in the motion picture industry that transpired just after the installation of the first sound equipment on film sets.

On October 9, 1927, a mediocre movie called *The Jazz Singer* opened on Broadway. In this opus the Jewish blackface singer, Al Jolson, punished a piano, sang "Mammy," and swapped sweet talk with his fictional Yiddish Momma in a surprise scene from which most film historians date the demise of the "silents."

Although other pictures had lately been made with outsized sound effects, this single scene, stuck in the center of an otherwise silent stinker, shook up millions of fans, scared hell out of Hollywood producers, and sent a gaggle of "silent" stars, unable to speak the King's English, scurrying to drama coaches who'd lately arrived from New York on the Santa Fe Super Chief, hoarse as crows from cinders and desert dust after a four-day journey.

These cultural missionaries, having set up shop either in the old Hollywood Hotel or a nearby canyon, began teaching around the clock, while a few articulate stage and screen stars at Warner Brothers and Paramount kept a similar schedule, moving stiffly in cramped sound sets from a microphone hidden under a lamp's fringed shade to another cached in a leafy rubber plant.

Before the spring of 1929 a few good talkies were made, such as *The Doctor's Secret* with Broadway's honey-voiced Ruth Chatterton and Hollywood's H. B. Warner.

Like Evelyn Brent, who was featured in *The Lion and the Mouse*, and George Bancroft, who starred in *The Wolf of Wall Street*, Mr. Warner had successfully passed the sound tests.

So, too, had De Mille's greatest star, Gloria Swanson, who would soon be receiving critical plaudits for her poignant role in *The Trespasser*, and the beautiful Betty Compson, who would score with Eric von Stroheim (the Man You Love to Hate) and a dummy called Otto in a fine film about a mad ventriloquist entitled *The Great Gabbo*.

But these pioneers, blessed with good voices and acceptable diction, were in the minority, and most "silent" stars were scared to death of the microphone.

Helen Morgan's diction, both in song and speech, was impeccable, and she'd been using the mike since the early 1920s. Thus she was able to walk on the sound stage with less trepidation than most. But there was another reason why she could begin work on her first "talkie" without throwing up beforehand. And it concerned a young man Paramount had hired to direct *Applause*.

Five weeks before Helen reported for work, this young Theater Guild director, who had also once directed opera at Rochester, New York, turned up at the Astoria studio to watch some shooting and ask some questions "about lenses and things." Then, just after New Year's day of 1929, working with quiet confidence in a medium foreign to him, Rouben Mamoulian began to direct *Applause* and to stir up considerable dust on the set out there in Astoria.

In his first film, about an over-the-hill burlesque queen and her sheltered daughter, this young Armenian immigrant revo-lutionized the shooting technique in talkies.

Mamoulian yearned to employ a movable camera, but that didn't seem possible since camera, cameraman, director, and assistant cameraman were all cooped up in a "sort of house on wheels." They had only a single recording track and the micro-phone invariably picked up extraneous noises.

During his third day on the set, Mamoulian announced that he'd like to do, all in one shot, a scene wherein the daugh-ter lay in bed in a tawdry hotel room with her mother (Helen Morgan) beside her singing a burlesque song "as if it were a lullaby," while the girl, telling her beads, simultaneously whis-pered a prayer.

The technicians claimed that the song and the prayer couldn't be recorded on a single mike and one channel, so Mamoulian asked why they couldn't use two mikes and two channels and "combine the two tracks in printing."

The sound man and the cameraman swore it couldn't pos-sibly be done, so Mamoulian went up, furious, to producer Adolph Zukor's office. He complained that nobody downstairs would cooperate with him, so Zukor went down with him to the set and ordered the crew to do the thing his way.

The men became sullen, refusing to give the Armenian any help, so he tackled the project alone and saw to it that two takes were "in the can" by half past five.

That night a "secret screening" of the day's rushes was held in the studio projection room—and the results delighted Zukor, who had the takes rushed to a Paramount sales con-ference.

On the set next day, Rouben Mamoulian was greeted as Paramount's white-haired boy and listened to with respect. Everyone said he had to be wrong not to allow Helen Morgan to be glamorous; nevertheless, he had her made up and pad-ded to look like a tired, aging burlesque stripper, and, accord-ing to him, the reviews turned out to be "sensational."

That's the Mamoulian–*Applause* success story, and it's authentic except for one overstatement: Not all the reviews were "sensational."

In the *New York Times*, for instance, Mordaunt Hall mistakenly quibbled that the Theater Guild director "rather lets his penchant for camera feats run away with suspense." Then, happily unaware of attacking a future film classic, Hall ran on, "Mr. Mamoulian delights in swinging his camera back and forth and in many instances he does so with a certain effect," adding that though some scenes were "exceedingly well recorded," others were "lamentably tubby." ("Tubby" was a 1929 word that must have been the equivalent of 1970s' "sudsy.")

As to the picture's star, who'd previously played only one dramatic role on the stage and none on the screen, Hall employed a tone of guarded patronage: "Helen Morgan does remarkably well in the tried and true conception of a burlesque queen's existence. . . . Miss Morgan speaks her lines with feeling and plays her part with ability."

Meager praise indeed for the young Armenian director and his twenty-nine-year-old star, who, in a new medium, was matching her natural gifts against the talents of at least a dozen other stage and screen artists at Paramount.

Among the stage people who made their talking film debuts at Astoria were Claudette Colbert, Edward G. Robinson, Fredric March, Walter Huston, Miriam Hopkins, Jeanne Eagels, Tallulah Bankhead, the four Marx brothers, and Jeanette MacDonald. Out there, Miss Colbert made *The Barker*, Eddie Robinson played his first gangster in *The Hole in the Wall*, and Miss Eagels, fresh from her triumph in *Rain*, made *The Letter*, a picture adapted from another story by Somerset Maugham.

Yet of these ventures (and more), only one Paramount film and one star would be singled out by reviewers for unstinted praise during the 1967 New York Film Festival.

In that year, after viewing *Applause* at Philharmonic Hall, Howard Thompson, a *New York Times* drama critic, delivered himself of the following eulogy:

> *Applause* is a remarkable film technically even now. . . .
> As a pioneer venture in sound and show business photog-

raphy, the movie is boldly imaginative and effective. Acoustically and visually, the burlesque orbit has never seemed so authentic on the screen. And the reason for it— and may we never forget it—is Rouben Mamoulian.

Made principally in New York, this is a backstage drama of old-time burlesque, starring Helen Morgan as an aging, warm-hearted, singer-stripper trying to shield her convent-reared daughter from the tawdriness of her world . . . . As the long-suffering mother, Miss Morgan is entirely convincing. Mr. Mamoulian has seen to the rest.

There it was in black and white in the *Times* thirty-eight years after Mordaunt Hall, in the same paper, had made his critical gaffe. Now, *Applause* had finally earned for its director and star a measure of cinematic immortality.

The "remarkable" facts were obvious, after nearly four decades: in his first film Rouben Mamoulian had shown himself to be a sharply observant, technically creative director, and Helen Morgan, under his sensitive guidance, had created in her first film a memorable, three-dimensional central character.

In retrospect, Morgan's work schedule throughout this last year of the 1920s seems fantastic.

Since mid-January she had been going each night from the Ziegfeld Theater to the New Amsterdam Roof to appear in *Ziegfeld's Midnight Frolic*.

She went straight from *Show Boat*, in stage makeup, to the Roof, where she sang one number, did an encore, and appeared in a Ben Ali Haggin tableau.

At home Lulu always had a late-hours snack on the burner, and after she and her daughter had mulled over their separate activities during the day, Helen would go to her room to familiarize herself with the next day's shooting schedule at Paramount.

She made *Applause* while playing, each week, six evening performances and two matinées of *Show Boat*, plus six nightly cabaret stints in *Frolic*.

When *Show Boat* took to the road on May 6, she stayed in

New York to work in Paramount's *Glorifying the American Girl,* and possibly to rest up a bit before beginning rehearsals for a new Broadway musical.

Way back in 1917 she had worked as a singing waitress in a German beer garden next door to producer Jessie Bonstelle's Old Garrick Theater, and after a night's performance the stock company's leading ladies—Anne Harding and Kit Cornell—would sometimes drop by the garden to hear the sweet-voiced "little Morgan girl."

The garden was called Adeline's, and Helen's stories about her brief sojourn there must have inspired Kern and Hammerstein to create a musical play especially for her entitled *Sweet Adeline.* After six months of intensive work the boys had completed the book and score, and Helen rehearsed the show half the summer while maintaining her full *Show Boat*–New Amsterdam schedule.

As always, the preparation for a Broadway show was strenuous, but Morgan never really minded those weeks of tedious labor. She'd say, "Rehearsals are interesting and energizing. It's life outside the theater that's tiresome. Nothing to look forward to but the same old routine, day after day." And, of course, she could not have failed to rehearse *Adeline* with a constant surge of inner excitement.

This production, a musical romance in two acts and fifteen scenes, starring Helen Morgan, with book and lyrics by Oscar Hammerstein II and music by Jerome Kern, was almost a family affair.

The "book" was staged by Reginald Hammerstein, and the show, produced by Arthur Hammerstein, opened September 3 at Hammerstein's Theater downtown with a glittering first-night audience and most of the first-string critics present when the curtain rose on a beer garden, owned and operated by Addie's papa.

In the first scene Helen impressed a *New York Times* reviewer as looking "extravagantly beautiful" in a "coiling" 1890s gown while she sang, "in the pensive, gently melancholy mood" that "had long endeared her to the sympathetic citizenry out front, the overture number ' 'Twas Not So Long

Ago,' a waltz song called 'The Sun About to Rise,' and the haunting theme aria 'Here Am I.' "

In the play Addie goes from the New Jersey beer garden to rehearse a Broadway musical from which she'll emerge as a public idol. She gets involved with the show's backer but later falls in love with her composer (just like in real life, remember?) and (unlike real life) marries him to live happily ever after.

The scenes of the play shift from the beer garden to the New York rehearsal hall, to a Spanish American War hospital tent on San Juan Hill, then back to a Bowery burlesque theater and the "social bar" of the Hoffman House, an old Manhattan hotel.

Since no attempt was made to satirize the period, the cast played everything straight as they sang the dying soldier's ballad, "Just Break the News to Mother," then lightened the atmosphere with the ragtime rhythms of "Hello My Baby" and "A Bicycle Built for Two."

For some unknown reason Brooks Atkinson again failed to show up for a Morgan opening, but the nameless *Times* man who did extolled the entire production.

He was happy to report that Kern and Hammerstein had "especially composed" for Miss Morgan "those broken, tearful ballads" she sang "while perched on the nearest convenient shelf." Then, employing extraordinary insight, Mr. Anonymous came as near as anybody ever would to the baffling emotional effect Morgan always created, by concluding: "So *Sweet Adeline* not only uses her for its own purpose, but preserves the strange, submissive quality of her personality."

Charles Butterworth, who'd been with Helen in *Americana*, was now playing a "patiently aspiring young rake named Ruppert Day" who ended up as "the confused backer of a wavering show," and this critic decided that Butterworth would become "one of the drollest comedians of our time."

In fact this *Times* critic praised just about everybody in *Sweet Adeline*, including a blowzy Bowery diva played by Irene Franklin, and referred to the whole production as Kern and Hammerstein's "successor to the epochal *Show Boat* . . . a gay carnival unfolded with joy."

He said, "they have chosen a period again and garnished it with captivating music and decorated it with the fluent costumes and circular hats of the day." The mood, he said, "was less sentimental than gay"; the humor, as might have been expected, "sophisticated" but "exuberantly good-natured." The story was woven "delicately into a generous brocade of many delights," the rehearsal scene was "effortless and spontaneous," and, finally, running out of adjectives, the reviewer stated that *Sweet Adeline* was so "compact with sundry pleasures" that he could only say the whole production was "downright enjoyable all the while."

This was a rave review, of course, but all the critics' reactions were generally favorable.

Richard Lockridge found *Adeline* "A very pretty and lilting show." Percy Hammond sized it up as "a gentle opera. . . . A semi-serious and old-fashioned musical, one of the politest frolics of the year."

John Mason Brown spoke of its "moments of complete enjoyment," and Robert Littel proclaimed it "a grand and gorgeous show."

Adeline's advance ticket sale had been more than satisfactory. Now, after the morning and evening papers' reviews, long lines formed at the box office, and the house was sold out two months ahead.

Apparently New Yorkers and out-of-towners alike could not get enough of Kern and Hammerstein, Irene Franklin, Charles Butterworth, and, most of all, Helen Morgan, who sang to them (from "any convenient shelf"), in addition to the aforementioned three hit songs, the tender "Don't Ever Leave Me" and the dramatic torch number, "Why Was I Born, Why Am I Living?" These songs had been written just for Morgan, and she made the most of a long-delayed chance to shine in this musical as a touching actress, a unique *chanteuse*, and, finally, a dazzling star with her name in lights above the title of a Kern-Hammerstein success.

Adeline lilted and soared through an Indian summer September and twenty-eight golden days of October—right on up to Black Thursday, when the crash that struck Wall Street reverberated throughout the United States, Canada, England, and every city in the Western Hemisphere where American tourists were pursuing the '20s favorite pastime of wasting the easy-come Yankee dollar.

Sweet Adeline would succumb too soon for such an exceptional offering, but not without having achieved a respectable run.

If the crash hadn't come, this production might have challenged *Show Boat*'s record of 572 New York performances, with an average weekly gross of fifty thousand dollars.

Even so, with a national depression descending, the lovely show, thanks to a fine advance sale, lasted through 234 performances.

Helen was out of the cast from December 12 through December 15 with laryngitis, so her understudy, Eunice Tierney, had a chance to take over temporarily, as she once had, in *Show Boat*.

Christmas was coming and Miss Tierney probably would not have asked for a better present, but Helen was back on her "shelves" on December 16 and Eunice was back in a dressing room reading *Variety* and playing solitaire.

Crash or no crash, this was a joyous Yuletide season for Helen, Lulu, Jerome Kern, various Hammersteins, and everybody connected with a sold-out hit.

Great friendships formed during the run of *Show Boat* were now going extra strong. Jerry Kern had adored Helen from the night he discovered her in *Americana*. And as for Oscar Hammerstein, any restraint he may have felt because of Helen's "crush" on him had long since been forgotten. The boys could find no fault with their star, and Helen was not only grateful but proud to have justified the faith they had manifested in creating a show around a central character who was remarkably like herself. They had written five memorable songs for her, and she had repaid them for their pains by turning all five into hits.

Morgan would always remember the air of cheerful harmony that prevailed backstage during the run of this show—and it is significant to note, as proof of the mischievous backstage camaraderie she and her mother shared with Oscar and Jerry, that those two imps had named their over-the-hill Bowery diva Lulu.

8

Enter, George Blackwood

NOWADAYS, WHEN MOVIE PEOPLE may spend from one to three years on a major film, it seems remarkable that Helen Morgan made three Paramount pictures within a twelve-month period. The first of these to open on Broadway after *Applause* was *Glorifying the American Girl*, a "backstage" musical in which, according to the *New York Times*, "the only bright spots" were those in which Helen Morgan, Eddie Cantor, Rudy Vallee, and Mary Eaton appeared as *Follies* stars.

The other film was a melodrama called *Roadhouse Nights*, and the critics all liked it.

Mordaunt Hall praised Ben Hecht's script, Hobart Henley's direction, Jimmy Durante's "good low comedy," and Charles Ruggles' humorous portrayal of a newspaper man named Willie Bindbugle. Helen played Lola Fagin, a nightclub singer (what else?) who saved her old friend Bindbugle's life by gunning down the wicked roadhouse owner, and Hall said that she "sang agreeably and acted impressively," bringing to her role "a human interpretation."

Roadhouse Nights opened February 22, 1930, and the next day's papers carried a brief item stating that Helen, Charles Butterworth, and Irene Franklin would soon be on the road with *Sweet Adeline*. However, plans for this tour fell through (perhaps because of the rapidly developing depression) and Helen stayed in town to sing over radio station WEAF.

Adeline closed near the middle of March, and Helen opened at the Palace on March 30. This was her second turn at the grand old house, and this time none of the critics dared resort to faint praise. As was too often the case, the *Times'* reviewer had no byline, but he made it plain that somebody down there loved Helen. He began by saying, "Now that upper Broadway and the Hammerstein Theater are without a *Sweet Adeline* or anything like it, virtually no one can be astonished that Helen Morgan has been fetched south to the Palace as swiftly as possible."

After noting that the lady was "clearly annoyed by a cold," he went on to say her renditions of "Why Was I Born," "Bill," and "Here Am I" added up to "a fervent event . . . for when, in her most beguiling, between-you-and-me-fashion, she sings what Jerome Kern has composed, nothing else seems to matter very much. Miss Morgan—and now when you speak of Miss Morgan, you add, 'in person'—has a gift for nostalgic song and nothing can stop it from. being both expert and glamorous."

To Helen these were lovely words, indeed. Besides, this was a week to be remembered, for Jules Bledsoe, *Show Boat*'s original Joe, was on the bill singing "Ol' Man River" and it was wonderful to see and hear him again.

By a peculiar coincidence, a story just below the Palace review in the *Times* gave out the news that Paul Robeson, who within two years would play Joe in a revival of *Show Boat*, was making theatrical history in Berlin as the star of Eugene O'Neill's *The Emperor Jones*.

This was the first time a play in English by an American playwright, directed by and starring an American, had been presented in the German capital, and even without a program synopsis in German, the "enthusiastic" first-night audience at the Deutsches Kuenster Theater had found Robeson's acting "graphic enough to tell the story vividly." Thousands of Amer-

icans—including Helen Morgan—had yet to learn what he
could and would do two years later with Joe and "Ol' Man
River" on the opening night of a glittering *Show Boat* revival.

Helen rested this year throughout the late spring and early
summer, and it may be that her manager decided to keep her
name in the newspapers at any cost, since the *New York Times*
on August 9 announced that she would shortly be involved
with a project that must have astonished her friends.

Just how she came to be chosen queen of the annual New
Jersey Baby Parade is anybody's guess. Yet down to Ocean
City she went for her coronation on the evening of August 21,
to be followed by other shenanigans next day.

Now, all women who aren't by nature psychopathic mon-
sters are supposed to love babies, and Miss Morgan had nothing against them, but she did share with her idol, Ethel
Barrymore, a conviction that no actress should ever appear on
stage with a child or a dog. Any script with a bright kid or a
darling puppy in its cast was usually returned unread by these
ladies with the cryptic notation "Not interested at this time."
Accordingly, it may well have been that the Morgan smile
throughout this two-day ordeal grew faintly strained toward
sunset on August 22.

She came back to town to rehearse for a more adult project
the following week, and the *Times* carried a portrait of her
on August 31 with an announcement of her next radio engagement. She appeared as guest artist on Friday, September 5, at
8:00 P.M. over station WJZ, "mingling new melodies with
old" in the first program of a new weekly series with Nat
Brusiloff's orchestra.

This meant money, all right, but still, here she was at summer's end with no new show in sight and no prospect of steady
work in the fall.

Actually, she would not work again until February 1931,
and she may have been not only apprehensive but frightened
in the fall of this first depression year.

Arthur Loew was very much in her life now, but it would
have been wholly unlike her to accept—much less ask—finan-

cial aid from him or any man while she had her health and
Arthur Benton as her friend and agent.

On February 2, 1931, the *Times* headlined Helen's third
appearance at the Palace—with the names of Phil Baker, Jay
C. Flippen, and Morton Downey in smaller print beneath her
own. The *Times* man reported that after she'd got off to a
"leisurely start" with a couple of less than highly distinguished
numbers, she began to "eat her heart out publicly" with the
old Kern and Hammerstein favorites from *Show Boat* and
Sweet Adeline.

After a single week at the Palace she was out of work until
mid-April, when she began to rehearse for Flo Ziegfeld.

As usual, the *Follies* tried out in Atlantic City, and this
year a South Seas Island sprite called Reri, who'd recently
caught the public's fancy in a film entitled *Tabu*, received
Ziegfeld's full publicity treatment.

Still, in the show's general publicity, the names of Helen
Morgan and Harry Richman appeared in larger print than
those of the other principals, who included such top performers as Ruth Etting, Gladys Glad, Jack Pearl, Hal Le Roy,
Frank McCormick—and, incidentally, an unknown teenager
from Los Angeles who'd changed her name from Mitzi Ger-
ber to Mitzi Mayfair before setting out on a stage and film
career that would cover forty years.

Mr. Z had culled three Texas charmers from the Galveston
beauty contest, and Atkinson found them "demure and well
mannered" as they whirled about—"sometimes in fluffy gowns
but more frequently with a low percentage of coverage." They
also appeared as cabaret dancers and bright-feathered Indi-
ans, rivaled in presentation only by five languorous beauties
who reclined on the tusks of as many live elephants.

Noel Coward had written a number called "Half-Caste
Woman" especially for Helen Morgan, but the regretful con-
sensus seemed to be that this year (like the Damon Runyon
character Nicely, Nicely) the lady was "back on Broadway
doing the best she could—which was no better than somewhat," with special material that wasn't quite right for her.

Atkinson made short shrift of nearly everyone in the cast,

plus the material they had to work with. He described the show as "a big well-staged revue" hampered by "a bankruptcy of ideas" that merely added up to "good summer entertainment."

Like other critics, Atkinson noted Reri's "natural beauty," adding that her "native dancing" had "the grace and rhythm of a woodland waterfall."

In retrospect, the attention Atkinson and his colleagues paid to this little South Seas nymph who, after the final curtain on opening night, ran up Fifty-fifth Street toward Seventh Avenue with an armful of flowers like an excited child, presaged a sadly familiar Broadway story.

After the run of this show, Reri would disappear from the limelight, while Helen Morgan would move on to earn fresh laurels for herself in a splendid revival of *Show Boat*.

Meanwhile, Helen was heartened by a pleasant turn of affairs when the old indictment against her and Texas Guinan was *nolle prossed* by Assistant Attorney Arthur Schwartz because, as reported in the *Times*, "circumstances made further prosecution out of the question."

This year, having played one week at the Palace and ten in the *Follies*, Miss Morgan, while happily looking forward to another Ziegfeld production, could afford to shop without skimping for a lavish Yuletide at home.

In late December 1927 critic Alan Dale had predicted that *Show Boat* would "have a wonderful sail—no storms, no adverse winds, nothing to keep it from making port, goodness knows where."

Dale's insight had proved correct, for the road production that opened in Boston in May 1929 had played everywhere to packed houses on a ten month cross-country tour ending in the last days of March 1930.

By late winter 1932 Ziegfeld's plans for the revival had got under way with only two major changes in his original cast. By the time contracts were being drawn up, Mr. Z had signed Paul Robeson for the role of the dock worker, Joe, and Dennis King as Gaylord Ravenal. But there was another, trickier

problem to be solved. For, just after the opening, a replacement had to be found for Charles Ellis, who was playing Steve
Baker opposite Morgan's Julie. (Ellis had agreed to play
through the opening week on Broadway, after which he had
to join his wife, Norma Mitchell, in a show that would take
to the road.)

Ellis had worked well with Helen, and she was concerned
about a replacement since the melodramatic bloodletting
scene depended so much on split-second timing and fervid
emotional projection.

Ziegfeld's scouts were searching the town and beating the
sticks for a new leading man, but neither Mr. Z nor Miss M
was entirely satisfied with any aspirant who'd read for the
part.

Then, on a Saturday night in March, Ziegfeld's secretary,
Goldy McGinty, turned up with some friends at the Princeton
University Playhouse to see *Elizabeth the Queen*, with Eliza-
beth Risdon as the aging monarch and a tall, dark-haired
young actor named George Blackwood as the youthful Lord
Essex.

Watching the play, Goldy McGinty was fascinated by the
diverse emotions Blackwood revealed in his role, as indeed
she might have been, for when he'd replaced Alfred Lunt in
this part opposite Lynn Fontanne on Broadway, Alexander
Woollcott had said, "George Blackwood as Lord Essex, a
tremendously dramatic part, plays it as a true artist and gives
it great dramatic value."

After the play Goldy went backstage to congratulate the
handsome six-foot leading man and tell him about the search
for a *Show Boat* leading man to play opposite Helen Morgan.
She left the dressing room saying, "Don't be surprised if you
get a call from Mr. Ziegfeld."

Elizabeth the Queen moved on to Newark, then switched
back to Boston, where it closed on the second Saturday after
its Princeton stand.

George Blackwood returned to his New York apartment
on Sunday, spent a convivial "long time no see" evening with
friends, and woke the next morning to reach out blindly for a

shrilling telephone. The call was from Goldy, who told him that Mr. Ziegfeld would like to see Mr. Blackwood that afternoon.

At the Ziegfeld Theater George made his way to the producer's sumptuous second-floor suite where, to his astonishment, he met not only the Fabulous Flo but Jerry Kern, Oscar Hammerstein II, Edna Ferber, scenic designer Joseph Urban, and costume designer John Harkrider.

Someone gave him a folder of sides and told him to step into an outer office and read over the bloodletting scene. Then, after about ten minutes, Miss Ferber (who, it would later transpire, had certain misgivings about this revival) came in to ask, "Are you ready, Mr. Blackwood?"

George said, "Well, I hope so, but I'm awfully nervous, Miss Ferber."

Edna told him that was to be expected but he really shouldn't be because all the gang in the inner office had agreed that he looked the part. Then she added, "Mr. Ziegfeld asked Goldy to read the sheriff's lines with you, but she begged off, so he drafted me. All I can say is, I'll do the best I can."

George felt slightly comforted by Edna Ferber's remarks, and somehow he managed to get through the scene without breaking up, even though the ever-stagestruck Ferber, employing a Deep South accent, gave all she had to the Mississippi sheriff.

At the end of the reading there was a moment's silence, then Mr. Z leaned forward in his leather chair and asked in his plangent voice, "Mr. Blackwood, would you mind waiting out in the reception room for just a few minutes?"

George said, "Of course, sir," and left the office shaken.

In the outer room he sank weakly into a chair and waited, dripping sweat, for more than twenty minutes. Then the door opened and Miss McGinty, smiling broadly, asked him to step back into the sanctum.

All the seated judges were smiling now, and Ziegfeld beamed up at him, saying, "We were all extremely pleased by your reading, Mr. Blackwood. Now I wonder if you'd mind—just as a courtesy, though it isn't really necessary—going over to read the scene with Miss Helen Morgan at the St. Regis?"

Blackwood's heart leaped as he answered, "I'd be happy to Mr. Ziegfeld," and he rose to leave, extremely excited, not only by getting the part of Steve but by the prospect of meeting a woman he'd always admired.

Outside, he crossed Sixth Avenue and struck off, with his long, loping stride, up Fifty-fifth Street toward the hotel's familiar portico.

High up in her St. Regis suite Miss Morgan, after a call from Flo, had brushed her hair, dabbed on some makeup, and slipped into a trailing magenta hostess gown.

As someone tapped on the door she called, "Who is it, please?" And a deep voice answered, "My name's George Blackwood. Mr. Ziegfeld sent me."

Morgan skipped to the door, opened it, undid the protection chain, and smiled up at the handsome six-foot Ohioan as she bade him enter.

She held out her slim white hand and told him, "I'm glad to see you, Mr. Blackwood. Flo said you were very good-looking, but he didn't mention that voice."

Helen seated herself on a small sofa, talking fast. "Now, just sit down here and tell me all about what you've done in the theatre while I hum some scales. I'm singing here in the Continental Lounge and I have to warm up my voice for tonight's first show."

George launched into a brief résumé, unsure that Morgan was hearing a single word through her airy humming, but when he'd finished she nodded and told him, "That's fine, Mr. Blackwood. Oh, hell, why don't I call you George and you call me Helen? Now, George, let's run through the scene you did for Flo. I'll read the part of the sheriff."

She picked up a silver letter opener from a small table by the sofa and gave it to George. "This is your prop. Now, right from the start I want to see in your face and eyes that you're hearing this back-country lout and his nigger-hating, drunken gang on the levee shouting, 'God damned white bastard, mar-

ried to a nigger wench. Shoot him, and throw his stinking
carcass to the filthy sows.' "

Astonished by Morgan's deep-voiced vehemence, George
reacted as she'd told him to while she muttered, "Here, grasp
my hand and turn the palm out toward the audience. That's
right. Now cut my right forefinger, bend over, and suck the
blood. Yes. That's it exactly. Now, hear them breaking the
door in and stand up tall and defiant. That's it, *yes*. That's
right. *Now*, let's have your first line."

George said, "I'm Steve Baker and this is my wife." Then
Morgan, as the bayou sheriff, rumbled, "You two better dress
and come along with me."

By this time, doubling as the sheriff and Julie Dozier,
Helen was in George's arms as he declaimed over her head,
"You wouldn't call a man a white man that's got Negro blood
in him, would you?"

On cue, Morgan stepped back, growling, "No, I wouldn't.
Not in Mississippi. One drop of nigger blood makes you a
nigger in these parts."

George drawled, "Well, I got more than a drop of nigger
blood in me, and that's a fact."

The pseudo-sheriff scowled up at him, fearsomely. "You
ready to swear to that in a court of law?"

"I'll swear to it any place," George answered, lifting his
head. "Look at all these folks here. There ain't one of 'em but
can swear I got nigger blood in me this minute. That's how
white I am."

As the last deep, resonant note of his voice died out, Morgan looked at him, nodding. Then she floated off to a desk,
picked up the phone, gave the operator a number, and waited.

She was smiling at Blackwood over the phone, and all at
once that white smile widened as she said into the mouthpiece, "Flo, I have found my Steve."

George left the St. Regis, floating. Like everyone else who'd
ever been hired for a Ziegfeld show, he was overwhelmed by
the prospect of working for the great impresario, let alone
playing a riverboat leading man to this glamorous star.

Helen as she looked shortly after being selected Miss Mount Royal for Montreal's Winter Sports Festival of 1918. (*Culver Pictures*)

A studio portrait of Helen taken when she was appearing in *Americana*. (*Culver Pictures*)

Jerome Kern, composer of the music for *Show Boat* and the man most responsible for Helen's rise to stardom. (*Wide World Photos*)

Florenz Ziegfeld, the fabled showman and impresario who produced the original stage version of *Show Boat* in 1927 and the Broadway revival in 1932. (*Pictorial Parade*)

Helen as Julie in the original *Show Boat* production. (*Culver Pictures*)

Mabel Walker Willebrandt, assistant United States attorney general in charge of enforcing prohibition laws. Her campaign against New York's most popular speakeasies resulted in Helen Morgan's 1928 arrest for violation of prohibition law. (*Wide World Photos*)

Texas Guinan, ebullient hostess at the 300 Club, also arrested in 1928 for violation of prohibition law. (*Wide World Photos*)

Arthur Loew, the first man in Helen's life, as he appeared in 1932. (*Wide World Photos*)

Helen (right) and Joan Peers in *Applause*, Helen's first motion picture, which has since come to be regarded as a movie classic.

Helen with Jimmy Durante in *Roadhouse Nights* (1930).
(*Culver Pictures*)

George Blackwood, who
became Helen's lover while
touring with her in the
road company version of
Show Boat. (*Courtesy
George Blackwood*)

Blackwood as Steve Baker in the road company version of *Show Boat. (Courtesy George Blackwood)*

An early photograph of Myrtle Bell ("Mother") Blackwood, later to become a close friend of Helen's. *(Courtesy George Blackwood)*

HANNA THEATRE

Under the Direction of

THE HANNA THEATRE COMPANY

John S. Hale Manager

"The Playhouse with the Atmosphere of Friendliness"

The HANNA Theatre is represented in New York by the
UNITED BOOKING OFFICE, Inc.
Which books both the Shubert and Erlanger and Associated Attractions
for this theatre.

WEEK BEGINNING MONDAY DECEMBER 26 1932
Matinees Wednesday and Saturday

HELEN MORGAN

in

ZEIGFELD PRODUCTION
AMERICA'S MUSICAL ROMANCE

SHOW BOAT

Aadapted from the novel by Edna Ferber

Music by
JEROME KERN

Book and Lyrics by
OSCAR HAMMERSTEIN II

Scenes by Joseph Urban Costumes Designed by John Harkrider

George Hirst, Musical Director

This Theatre, under normal conditions, with every seat occupied, can
be emptied in less than three Minutes. Look around now, choose
the nearest Exit to your seat, and in case of disturbance, WALK
(do not run) to that Exit.

Program for The Hanna Theatre Company presentation of Helen
Morgan in *Show Boat* for the week of December 26, 1932.

CAST

Windy	A. Alan Campbell
Steve	George Blackwood
Pete	James Swift
Queenie	Angeline Lawson
Parthy Ann Hawks	Bertha Belmore
Cap'n Andy	William Kent
Elly	Peggy Cornell
Frank	Harland Dixon
Rubber Face	Francis X. Mahoney
Julie	HELEN MORGAN
Gaylord Ravenal	Paul Keast
Vallon	Thomas Gunn
Magnolia	Margret Adams

You Belong to Me (1934). Helen assumes a familiar pose. (*Wide World Photos*)

With Ned Sparks in *Marie Galante* (1934). (*Culver Pictures*)

With Rudy Vallee in *Sweet Music* (1935). (*Culver Pictures*)

Helen and first husband, Maurice Mashke, a few months after their June 1935 divorce. (*Wide World Photos*)

At her nightclub the House of Morgan, in a gown she designed
herself (1936). (*Wide World Photos*)

Sammy White chats with Helen during the filming of *Show Boat* (1936). Because her dress was so tight and so equipped with bustles, this leaning ironing board provided Helen's only means of relaxing between takes. (*Culver Pictures*)

Singing "Can't Help Lovin' That Man" in the Ziegfeld version
of *Show Boat*. (*Culver Pictures*)

With Irene Dunne in the Universal Studios film version of *Show
Boat*. (*Culver Pictures*)

Helen, cheerfully en route to Europe in 1937. (*Wide World Photos*)

Helen and her second husband, Lloyd Johnson, sit on a piano at Miami Beach preparatory to cutting the wedding cake at the reception following their marriage (July 27, 1941). (*Wide World Photos*)

Mrs. Lulu Morgan and Lloyd Johnson at the funeral service for Helen, held at St. Francis Xavier Roman Catholic Church in LaGrange, Illinois (October 11, 1941). (*Wide World Photos*)

(*Wide World Photos*)

9

Show Boat *Revival*

BLACKWOOD COULD NOT, of course, conjecture as to how the past half-hour's interview had affected Helen Morgan, but she would tell him, much later, when they were close friends, what she'd done when the door closed behind him.

Still smiling, light as air inside, she'd hurried to her portable bar, poured herself a dash of brandy, and sat down again on the sofa. She was relieved to have found her new stage partner, but more than that she sensed that she might also have found a potential friend in this almost incredibly handsome young fellow whose awed admiration for her had been so plain in his eyes.

Loneliness was a fearsome ogre that Helen could never bear to face. She was often aware of that ogre's presence, and even though she'd been singing lately to appreciative crowds in the St. Regis Lounge, she'd loathed coming up in the early morning hours to this luxurious suite where no one awaited her.

She would not have been staying here if she hadn't decided, when Lulu left town to spend a month with friends in Montreal, to sublease the Fifty-fourth Street apartment to her osteopath, Dr. Edward Chagnon.

Without Lulu, this public favorite who sang each night to rounds of sustained applause—this woman who drank with convivial friends—almost always felt alone and desolate.

She was faced with the prospect of putting in another fortnight at this hotel, and every morning near daybreak she'd be

left alone with her thoughts and a snifter of brandy. This was
the way it had to be, since casual sexual encounters were not
for her. Besides, she was in love with Arthur Loew, now, and
even at times such as this when her man was out of town, she
had no inclination to bed down with anyone else.

Two more weeks must be endured before she and Lulu
would be back in their own place and she'd be rehearsing with
this new young man who had impressed her so much. She
had to get through them somehow, in solitary discontent.

Helen Morgan sighed and got up to replenish her glass,
once more dolefully humming her scales.

Show Boat's rehearsals began in April at the Earl Carroll
Theater, which Ziegfeld had rented even though he couldn't
sign a lease with the owner before the end of June.

The early rehearsals, in the afternoons, turned out to be
generally smooth despite the trio of new performers and the
extra hours Helen had to put in, after a full run-through,
going over her scenes with Blackwood.

Throughout any schedule of rehearsals Helen seldom took
a drink, even at a lunch break. And anyway, now that she
was once more involved, not only with Julie but with a stun-
ningly handsome, agreeable leading man, she felt no need to
sneak small nips from a bottle of old Three-Star Hennessy
stashed in her dressing room.

In the first week Mr. Ziegfeld was not out front as often as
he'd been in 1927, but of course then it had been easier for
him just to run down from his office in the New Amsterdam
to watch and let off an affectionate mock blast designed to
liven a lagging company's spirits.

Perhaps, though, if the original cast members hadn't been
preoccupied with their roles, someone might have noticed that
the Great White Father, when he did show up, was looking
considerably thinner and older as these spring days slipped
away.

Mr. Z had been confined to his hotel room with influenza
in Pittsburgh during the tryout of his *Hotcha* there in March.

However, he'd made a quick recovery, so nobody now at the Earl Carroll noticed any serious physical changes in the boss, nor even the air of absent preoccupation with which he occasionally viewed the rehearsals.

Plainly, *Show Boat* was about to set sail again with everything shipshape as before. And as for George Blackwood, the arduous, exacting afternoon hours sped on wings as he sat listening and watching this magical revival.

He'd been pleasantly surprised, after the first day's work, when Helen Morgan had asked him to walk with her to the hotel and have a drink. After that, the drink, and usually dinner, had become a ritual, and as the busy last days of April and early May passed, he and Helen became almost inseparable companions.

At the rehearsals' half-hour break George reintroduced his lady to Horn and Hardart's at Broadway and Forty-sixth Street, and the elegant Miss Morgan, who hadn't set foot in an Automat since her first lean year in town, dropped coins in the slots with a child's expectant delight.

She called the place Las Vegas—because, she said, "You know, George, when you drop in nickels and dimes here, it's like playing those damned machines—you never know what may happen. I mean, if you make a mistake in the slot you could be surprised by chopped chicken liver, instead of ham which maybe you just *thought* you wanted."

In the first weeks of work at the Earl Carroll there were no night rehearsals, so George proudly escorted Helen to seven Broadway productions. Together, in the best seats, they saw Ethel Waters in *Rhapsody in Black*; Laurette Taylor, at a Saturday matinée, in *Alice Sit by the Fire*; Katherine Cornell in *Lucrece*; Grace Moore in *The DuBarry;* Beatrice Lillie in *Walk a Little Faster*; Fred Astaire and Claire Luce in *The Gay Divorce*, and young Katharine Hepburn in *The Warrior's Husband*.

Helen's light-hearted reactions to three of these stars have stayed with Blackwood for forty years and even now he can recall them, word for word.

She said, "Darling, that Laurette Taylor's the greatest thing since Bernhardt, and I ought to know for I've *seen* Bernhardt."

Watching Claire Luce in her riotous over-the-chairs-and-sofa routine with the agile Fred, Morgan sighed, shaking her head as she murmured, "A body like that *and* starring with Fred Astaire: I mean, it's almost too much for any one woman to have."

In regard to Miss Hepburn, she widened her eyes as she whispered, "This girl's more masculine than the guy who's playing her husband. And judging from *that* accent, you'd think ancient Greece was located somewhere near Boston."

Helen was happier now than she'd been for a long time, working and playing with George. And long before the revival opened, she'd discover, after a few necking sessions, that she'd met a sexually attractive, virile, yet gentle male whom she might consider taking on as a lover. But still she was not quite sure she wanted to "go all the way" with George. Present or absent, Arthur Loew was her man. Besides, Lulu hadn't come home yet, and Helen felt compelled to have her practical mother size up this beguiling new companion.

She was grateful that George hadn't tried to force the sex issue and, even though she was puzzled by his restraint, she decided not to risk spoiling a possible future relationship by discussing the situation.

What the lady had no way of knowing was that Mr. Blackwood, who'd been experienced in various ways of love since he was sixteen, had no intention of pushing his luck with this beautiful, desirable woman who for some crazy reason seemed to be playing a coy game of hard to get. Anyhow, he felt privileged enough to be seen on Broadway with Helen Morgan, to be cast as her leading man, and, especially, to ride up with her in the St. Regis cage elevator after her last show in the lounge, to sip a nightcap and make light love on the sofa.

Blackwood had never lacked for sexual fulfillment; furthermore, his was a well-adjusted personality, due to a sheltered childhood in Canton, Ohio.

He was an experienced Broadway actor—having made his

debut in the spectacular production *Aphrodite* and gone from that, at sixteen, into the role of the queen's page, supporting Ethel and John Barrymore in the ill-fated *Clair de Lune*, which Mrs. Jack Barrymore wrote under the name of Michael Strange and for which she and the Barrymores were rewarded with scathing reviews, not the least hilarious of which was a write-up headlined: "For the Love of Mike."

After this fiasco George was co-starred with Dorothy Gish in Phillip Barry's *Holiday* at Philadelphia's Adelphi Theater, and no less a literary star than F. Scott Fitzgerald, subbing for the *Enquirer*'s regular reviewer, had written, "He gave a sparkling performance in a difficult leading male role."

Blackwood went on to play with Alice Brady in John Masefield's *The Witch*, with the magnificent Laurette Taylor in *Sweet Nell of Old Drury*, in Pinero's *The Enchanted Cottage*, Booth Tarkington's *Bristol Glass*, and A. A. Milne's *The Romantic Age*. He worked for two seasons as leading man with Jessie Bonstelle's stock company, toured as the male lead of *Death Takes a Holiday*, and, for a year and a half, played opposite Elizabeth Risdon in *Elizabeth and Essex*, before Goldy McGinty found him at the Princeton University Playhouse.

All these facts had been known to Edna Ferber and Flo Ziegfeld, as they undoubtedly were to Helen Morgan, but they were not so important to Helen as the sympathetic understanding George Blackwood had for the small, frightened girl who'd been raised near the railroad yards in Danville and on the West Side of Chicago.

George had grown up with his parents and a single enchanting sister, well fed, in a harmonious household on an Ohio farm, but that did not prevent his understanding the early struggle and actual hunger that Helen had shared with Lulu in the tough years after Tom Morgan's defection.

Then, too, he and Helen shared an unusual boon in their choice of maternal parents. Despite his father's skeptical attitude toward show business, George had come to New York at sixteen accompanied by Myrtle Bell Blackwood, who wanted to see that her son was properly settled in some decent place before he began the rigorous rounds of theatrical casting offices. And Lulu Morgan, of course, had never failed to encourage her lovely, talented daughter.

These two women, eschewing the aggressive drive of typical "stage mothers," nevertheless viewed the theatre, not as the devil's workshop but as the natural habitat of their comely offspring, and George and Helen, comparing anecdotes, couldn't wait for a possible future day when Myrtle Bell and Lulu could be brought together.

Therefore, as soon as she and Lulu were back in their apartment, Helen told Blackwood one afternoon at rehearsal, "I can't wait any longer to have you meet Mama. I'm going to call her right now."

She went to the backstage wall phone and George listened, amused, as she rattled away, "Mama, I'm bringing my new leading man home for dinner. Please order a nice centerpiece from that Rosary florist's place, put on one of your pretty new party dresses we bought at Arnold's . . . and, oh yes, honey, I think this just might be a good time to use the new Tiffany china and flatware."

When the two young people reached the Fifty-fourth Street flat, the floral piece, flanked by lighted tapers, had been centered on the establishment's best lace tablecloth.

Helen introduced George to Lulu, who eyed him appreciatively as her daughter excused herself, "to change."

On the way to her bedroom Helen paused to place a silver tray laden with her old Napoleon brandy, a siphon bottle, three crystal glasses, and a bottle of Lulu's Moxie on the living room's cocktail table, and Lulu asked Mr. Blackwood to be seated.

After a moment's talk about the weather, she asked, "May I call you George?" and Blackwood answered, "Yes, if I may call you Lulu. You're too young and good-looking to be addressed as Mrs. Morgan."

That was the proper opening gambit, all right, because Lulu *was* still a handsome woman, and straitlaced though she might be, she could not fail to react to the likes of this engaging ex-Ohio farm boy.

Helen returned to the living room wearing one of her filmy hostess gowns, and conversation flowed while the young people drank two highballs and Lulu sipped her Moxie.

Then Mother Morgan rose regally and said in a pleasant but no-nonsense tone, "Now, children, let's not spoil my dinner."

She wore a frilled apron over her new frock and, as she led the way to the dining table, George saw Helen pantomime the act of untying strings.

Lulu flushed and said, "Oh, excuse me, dears," as she took off the apron, and George seated her at the head of her table.

The lavish meal was expertly prepared, and after many compliments, George asked, "Lulu, where did you learn to cook like this?"

The lady answered, "Well, dear, I can assure you it wasn't in that lunchroom near the Canadian Pacific Railroad's roundhouse."

Blackwood had won Lulu's heart by praising not only her cooking but her trim figure, her manner of dress, her lively sense of humor. And Helen, sensing that George was sincerely impressed by her mother, listened and laughed with delight as the two chaffed each other.

Throughout the last weeks of rehearsal George was almost always at the apartment for early brunch, for dinners and numerous nightcaps—and Helen Morgan, enjoying the mutual admiration of two people who also loved and admired her, romped through these days and nights, laughing and never lonely.

On April 29, when Ziegfeld had signed a lease for the Earl Carroll, he hired workmen to paint and chisel out all the Carroll insignia, and long before the revival's dress rehearsals the marquee lights were flashing, Ziegfeld's Casino.

Show Boat opened to a full house swarming with bejeweled socialites, café society fans of Helen Morgan, screen and stage favorites, gay boys, lesbians, and a generous representation of jes' plain folks.

This heterogeneous audience also included many 1927 first-nighters who, remembering Jules Bledsoe as Joe, sat skeptically awaiting Paul Robeson's appearance as that articulate black dock worker. But something spectacular happened on this night of May 19, 1932, as Robeson came on to render "Ol' Man River." The carriage trade audience rose, shouted, stamped, and applauded him for nearly five minutes in an unprecedented ovation. Then, as his last cavernous note rang out, shivering the rafters, the show stopped cold.

Robeson repeated his performance, stopped the proceedings again, and finally left the stage, only to be called back time and again while the crowd's bravos drowned the attempted speeches of other players who were supposed to follow him.

Paul Robeson finally had to stand there and wait until *Show Boat*'s first-night audience would allow him to leave the Casino's stage so that the play might go on.

On May 15 all the critics reveled in joyous agreement, and none was more explicit than Brooks Atkinson about this revival.

He began by saying that he hoped Mr. Ziegfeld would make up his mind to keep on reviving *Show Boat* until Doomsday, and from there on, threw his hat in the air.

> After four and one-half years it still seems like a thoroughbred; it is still the most beautifully blended musical show we have had in this country . . . . readers with no stomach for superlatives had best abandon this review immediately . . . . for this is to be a fervent endorsement of the rhapsodies that sang all through the New York press during that bountiful Christmas week of 1927.

He went on, exulting, "*Show Boat* still has magic and loveliness; it is still warm and fragrant with sentiment." Praising Dennis King's "splendid voice" and "romantic manner," Atkinson said that both he and Robeson were "excellent substitutions," then really let himself go:

> _ Mr. Robeson has a touch of genius. It is not merely his voice, which is one of the richest organs on the stage. It is his understanding that gives "Ol' Man River" an epic lift. When

he sings it out of the cavernous depths of his chest, his face is a mask for the humble patience of the Negro race and you realize that Jerome Kern's spiritual has reached its final expression.

Atkinson said the rest of the cast members were "perfectly mated," and after tossing brief bouquets to Norma Terris, Charles Winninger, Edna May Oliver, and the comedy team of Eva Puck and Sammy White, he made up, *this* time around, for having dealt lukewarmly with Helen back in that 1927 Christmas week: "As the belle with Negro blood in her veins Helen Morgan retains the suppliant melancholy that captivates an audience and the expression of voice that turns resignation into beauty."

Atkinson wound up by praising Flo Ziegfeld for having "produced all this with a pride in craftsmanship," but his ultimate conclusion was that, just as much as Kern and Hammerstein, "these players"—in setting a tone of simple humor, romance, and friendliness—were responsible for the current "priceless achievement."

One week later, when Blackwood took over as Steve Baker, the New York *Daily News* critic Danton Walker told his readers, "The scene in which Julie is discovered to have black blood was played with flawless delicacy by Miss Helen Morgan and George Blackwood. He is a fine, romantic Steve, backed by a powerful stage presence and a commanding voice."

10

Exit, Mr. Ziegfeld

Show Boat WAS BACK, alive, and lustrous, but no critic, no friend, not even his wife, had any idea of the toll the revival of *Show Boat* had taken of Flo Ziegfeld's mental and physical stamina. At opening night there had been no sign of serious deterioration in his general health, but three days later a short item in the *Times* revealed some astonishing facts. On May 20 the House of Flowers, at 4 West 56th Street, filed a Supreme Court suit for some $1,267 against Ziegfeld. It seemed that on May 9, 1931, during the *Follies* rehearsals, the producer had signed a promissory note with the flower shop's manager for $786.50, and before the month of July was over he'd run up a bill at the "House" amounting to $480.85. About $130 of this had been spent on floral boxes sent to Lily Damita, a former *Follies* beauty, to Mrs. Billie Burke Ziegfeld, and to Gladys Glad, a principal in the *Follies* of 1931.

More significantly, $350 worth of orchids and roses had gone into a funeral piece for Helen Walsh, a former *Follies* chorine who had died of burns incurred in a yacht explosion —and to any discerning friend of Ziegfeld's, this newspaper item was more than revealing.

Billie Burke was on the road this summer in *The Vinegar Tree*, traveling with her daughter Patricia, and frequent floral boxes, as well as daily telegrams, were preceding Mr. Z's "two darlings" at every theater the play was booked into from Chillicothe, Ohio, to Santa Monica, California.

As to the other recipients of costly bouquets, Lily Damita was a Latin lady given to tantrums, and Gladys Glad may have been Mr. Z's current extramarital interest, but certainly the lavish floral piece for Helen Walsh, a chorine, was proof enough of Ziegfeld's concern for a lesser employee.

All these extravagant gestures were understandable. The puzzling point was this: How could a man who'd made, lost, and retrieved repeated fortunes since his first *Follies* in 1907 now be plagued by a florist's suit that included a promissory note for a mere $786.50?

Billie Burke knew that her husband had dropped more than a million dollars in the great crash, and that he'd gone into debt to the tune of $300,000 for *Smiles,* starring Marilyn Miller—but still, he had a success in *Hotcha,* this fabulous revival, and also the splendid radio show he was producing for Chrysler Motors. So how could he reasonably be in financial straits?

Actually, there were two factors that neither Ziegfeld's wife nor his physician suspected: The Pittsburgh bout with flu had seriously undermined Mr. Z's hardy constitution, and most of the box office take from this hit revival, above production costs and ample salaries, would be going henceforth to his creditors.

Meanwhile, to the people at the Casino, the Big Man seemed to be carrying on much as he always had. Complaints addressed to anyone connected with the production were still arriving in telegrams, when he could so easily have phoned the culprits from his Sixth Avenue office. And nobody failed to note his usual solicitous concern for his people, nor his special handling of Helen Morgan, who was really his outstanding star. It was as if he'd come to think of *her* as something precious to be kept wrapped in cotton wool. And even after forty years George Blackwood remembers Ziggy, knocking on Morgan's door, then poking his head inside to say, "It's raining out there, darling. Don't you want me to call a cab for you?"

It was noticeably true that the Great White Father looked rather older and even a little more tired than he had during rehearsals, but everyone realized he had two stage productions, plus this new Chrysler radio show to worry about. So it didn't seem odd that he wasn't quite his old self—especially during the present intense hot spell.

Throughout the last two weeks of May and the first half of June Helen Morgan and George Blackwood often shopped together and lunched downtown, or returned to Fifty-fourth Street for a special midday meal when Lulu felt like cooking. The two often dined at the St. Regis or Sardi's or a little Italian restaurant called Ralph's, and Lulu usually joined them on Saturdays at some pleasant place, between matinée and evening performances.

It was in June, too, that Helen introduced George backstage to a tall, dark eyed, well-tailored man with a prominent nose. This personage, who had sometimes sat out front during rehearsals, was, of course, Mr. Arthur Loew of M.G.M., and Helen had told George frankly that he was now, and had been since they met, the one man she hoped to marry.

George found him charming, but there were two puzzling things about the Morgan-Loew situation: why did Mr. Loew, who knew that Helen and George were now virtually inseparable, reveal no signs of jealousy? And why were the two never together except in Helen's dressing room?

By this time George had learned that Morgan could be coolly reticent about matters she didn't wish to discuss, so he refrained from asking personal questions.

Arthur Loew, however, was one of two men, besides George, about whom Helen felt strongly—in opposite ways—and Blackwood soon discovered that, as to the second one, whom he was soon to meet, she had no reticence at all.

One evening before a performance when George stuck his head in the door, she whirled about at the dressing table, left off talking with a good-looking middle-aged man, and sang out, "Come in, darling, and meet this old bastard who deserted me and my mother. George Blackwood, Tom Morgan."

As Morgan stood up, laughing, Blackwood gripped a muscular hand and found himself reacting favorably as almost everyone did to Tom's blue-eyed, ruddy-faced, smooth-tongued Irish charm. He was on vacation from his fireman's job on the Canadian Pacific Railroad, and he'd just come on to New York to see this daughter of his who'd made him and her mother so proud.

Amazingly, now that she was a star, Helen badgered and teased her old man with no trace of resentful bitterness, and George marveled at the easy camaraderie that seemed to exist between the two.

He was soon to learn, however, that Lulu Morgan's vehement reaction to her recalcitrant spouse was another thing. She had never forgiven Tom for leaving her twice during those desperately hard first years of Helen's babyhood, and she made absolutely certain during the fortnight he was in town that she would never run into him backstage.

All through this summer there were visitors, famous and otherwise, in Helen's dressing room, and none, besides Flo Ziegfeld, were more welcome than Kern and Hammerstein.

Oscar was always warmly amusing, and Jerry, who sometimes came back to launch mock-serious complaints against the chorus kids and the Jubilee Singers, always ended up by telling Helen, "But not you, honey baby. No sir, you're just perfect."

When Mr. Ziegfeld came back, he always acted pleased with the beautiful show—and so it seemed the boss and all his enterprises were going great guns.

Out on the West Coast, however, Billie Burke, listening one night in her Santa Monica living room to her husband's opening speech before a Chrysler show, heard a slight, quavering break in his voice and reacted with bone-chilled shock.

In the morning she made arrangements to leave California and boarded the earliest possible train with the teenaged Patricia.

In New York, even as she ran toward Ziegfeld's arms, Billie saw at a glance his lined, thin face and stooped shoulders. They went up to the Hastings-on-Hudson estate, where within a few days there were day and night nurses attending Mr. Z, who had suffered a relapse of flu, but he was declared out of danger on June 25.

On the second day of July two creditors who'd been unable to contact him in town or in the country had a Yonkers city court summons nailed to the front door of Burkeley Crest.

This action, brought by Charles E. McPartland and Bertram Keene of the Dobbs Ferry Grain Company, concerned a debt of which $908.27 was past due payment on a $2,780 note.

Billie Burke was dismayed by this omen of impending disaster. Then, after leaning over one night at the dinner table to feel her husband's pulse, she went straight to the phone and called Dr. Jerome Wagner, a nearby neighbor (and also husband to Norma Terris, who played Magnolia Ravenal).

Wagner came, examined Flo, then told his wife, "Rest. That will do it. Rest." And Mrs. Ziegfeld, who knew there would be no rest now for this man, either in town or at Burkeley Crest, lay awake that night planning an emergency course of action.

She drove into New York the next morning, made train reservations, bought three tickets, and arranged with Grand Central officials for the Ziegfelds to board the train at Harmon, New York, just a few miles from Hastings.

After that she took a cab to the Ziegfeld Theater and confided her plans to Goldy, to the switchboard operator, to Ziegfeld's manager, and to a girl who'd been acting as her own personal secretary, exacting promises from these trusted employees that no one else would be told where the Ziegfelds could be reached in California.

On the long, tedious journey westward, Billie, Patricia, and Ziegfeld's valet, Sydney, took turns packing pillow cases with ice so the sick man might have some relief from the fearful heat, but Mr. Z, weakened by pleurisy, remained half conscious all the way out.

In California, as in New York, Mrs. Ziegfeld avoided the press by getting her husband off the train at a small town called Barstow. She was gravely concerned, not only about his condition but about having to tell him, somehow, that on the way out she'd received a telegram saying his long-time general manager, Daniel Curry, had died.

Little Billie Burke drove with her party to her rented house in Santa Monica, where she received a phone call from Joseph Schenk offering his ranch as a convalescent retreat. However, when Ziegfeld became fully conscious he protested that he wanted to wait and talk to his dear friend Will Rogers, who was in Europe, about this whole situation, so the family stayed in Santa Monica.

As he grew stronger, the Great One resumed his extravagant practice of keeping in touch with everybody back East by phone and telegraph, running up, inside a month, a bill of six thousand dollars.

When he learned of Curry's death, he reacted with grievous shock, then rallied to call New York and persuade A. C. Blumenthal, husband of the ex-actress Peggy Fears, to take over as general manager with power of attorney to act in all Ziegfeld enterprises.

Planning, as his condition improved, to return to the Chrysler show in August, Ziegfeld worried about the July slump in *Show Boat*'s box office take. Then, when Miss Burke learned that he lacked money for salaries, she herself telephoned the wealthy Blumenthal, who personally guaranteed the necessary sum of twelve thousand dollars.

Billie hoped for the best now, but her husband grew steadily worse—and back east, people in the *Show Boat* cast who loved him read some shocking news on July 15.

On the previous day their beloved boss had been taken, gravely ill, to an unidentified sanitarium in New Mexico, where his wife told the press he "must not be disturbed by inquiries or messages from his friends."

On July 18 she had him removed to an unnamed Los Angeles hospital, and Dr. E. C. Fishbaugh reported that Mr. Z, who'd never fully recovered from a pleurisy attack sixteen weeks past, had, in the past few days, developed infections in both lungs. However, since his lately weakened heart had grown somewhat stronger, there was still hope for his recovery.

On Friday, after this news had appeared in the papers, George Blackwood sensed an atmosphere of ominous quiet backstage at the Casino, and as he entered Helen Morgan's dressing room, he found six ponies of brandy waiting for him on the makeup board.

Helen said, "As you can see, George, I'm ahead of you tonight."

While he dutifully downed the brandies, the two discussed the news, and, as they made their first entrance on stage, Steve realized that his "Julie" was weaving slightly. Of all the cast, no one except Norma Terris was as close to Ziegfeld as Helen—and certainly none was more apprehensive about his true condition.

She might well have been, too, since from this night on all the news about her "dear boss" would be bad, including a small item in the *New York Times* of July 20, which revealed that a judgment for unpaid taxes amounting to more than $300,000 had been filed against him.

In Hollywood director George Cukor told Mrs. Ziegfeld that she wouldn't be needed for about ten days at the studio where she was making *A Bill of Divorcement* with John Barrymore and Katharine Hepburn and, having already taken a room at the hospital, Billie stayed at Flo's bedside most of the time.

She had breakfast with him on the morning of July 22. At noon Patricia came with a lunch she'd fixed at home. And Flo, plainly neither nervous nor depressed, seemed much like his former self as the three ate and laughed together.

In the early afternoon Cukor called, apologetically, asking Billie to come out to the studio for a test with Walter Pidgeon, who might play her husband in the film.

At MGM Billie rehearsed the scene with Pidgeon. Then, as the cameras began to turn, Cukor suddenly halted the action and led her to a phone.

It was Sydney, the valet, speaking softly, "Come quickly, Madam."

A studio car sped Mrs. Ziegfeld to the hospital and the valet met her in the corridor, crying, "Oh, Madam, it's too late. He just died in my arms, walking across the room. One short gasp was all . . ." Then Sydney broke off in mid-sentence and sprang to catch his little madam as she sank toward the corridor floor.

This was at 10:15 in the evening. At the Casino Theater most of the show's cast and crew heard the dreadful news just after the final curtain, and the players' hands shook as they sat in their dressing rooms removing tear-streaked makeup.

When George Blackwood reached Helen's dressing room, he found her white-faced and still, holding a glass of brandy. The company manager looked in and she said, "Of course we won't go on tomorrow afternoon."

But the manager answered, "Yes, dear. Mr. Blumenthal thinks that's what Flo would want us to do."

Helen's gaze drooped as she nodded. "Yes, I guess that's right. Flo would expect us to."

From this moment on she seemed to be almost unnaturally controlled. At home with George and Lulu, she wept, but with no trace of hysteria. Grief was no stranger to Helen, and this night she seemed submissively resigned, facing the fact that death had come to an old, dear friend, even as it must come one day to everyone she'd ever loved, and to herself.

On July 23 the death of Florenz Ziegfeld made the front-pages of every Manhattan newspaper. The *Times* and the *Herald Tribune* ran two-column features with portraits and carefully detailed accounts of his full life story.

At the Casino, just before two o'clock, Blumenthal called the *Show Boat* company on stage and every eye turned toward Helen Morgan, who came on with George Blackwood.

She wore a small black hat with a nose veil, a black silk dress, and her necklace of matching pearls. The hat and dress were severely plain, but she had added the pearls for Flo, who had loved all rare, expensive things.

Standing stiff and straight beside George, she listened intently as Blumenthal assured the company that the show would definitely continue its run into the fall and begin a road tour after its closing in town.

Referring to the matinée, Blumenthal said in conclusion: "We are all shocked and saddened and we don't feel like singing or dancing, but Florenz Ziegfeld would want this show to go on, so it will go on as a tribute to him."

The cast members returned in silence to their dressing rooms. The call boys, as usual, stuck their heads in the doors, sounding the final warning, "Five minutes, Miss Morgan, Mr. King, Miss Terris, Mr. Robeson, Mr. Blackwood." Then it was time for the cast members to take their places in the wings.

At the end of the overture the curtain rose on the gala dockside scene in which Cap'n Andy introduced his players to the river-town folk out front. Then Charles Winninger, as the capering, dancing Cap'n, stepped out of character, walked to the footlights, and told the hushed audience with only a tiny quaver, "Ladies and gentlemen, the curtain will now be lowered for a moment of silence."

The house lights dimmed, the golden curtain slowly fell, and Ziegfeld's Casino went completely dark for an awesome sixty seconds.

Four people who respected and understood the inborn tenets of taste to which this great showman had always adhered had agreed on this gesture. They were Helen Morgan, Charles Winninger, the orchestra conductor, Paul Herst, and Peggy Fears Blumenthal.

After the matinée members of the cast chewed over scraps of news from the Ziegfeld office.

Flo's attorney, J. Arthur Levy, already had patrolmen guarding his office suite in the Ziegfeld Theater.

In Chicago old Mrs. Rosalie Ziegfeld, unconscious, as she had been for weeks, lay in her bed in the family mansion, mercifully unaware that her son's embalmed body had been placed in a Hollywood mortuary vault.

Out there Will Rogers, while making funeral and burial arrangements, had insisted on taking care of those expenses, saying to Billie Burke, "Flo loved me. Let me do this."

The following night at 10:30, over radio station WOR,

Blumenthal and some of the *Show Boat* principals would take part in a memorial program.

The front office staff had learned that a brief funeral service had been held that day in Hollywood, but no details were available at the time.

Backstage at the new Casino that evening, the orchestra men, the stage manager, and all the crew, as well as the cast, talked in hushed tones. The place had the air of a wake, and at the stage door each person, forcing a cheerful word for the sake of the sad old attendant, stepped out with shamed relief into the late golden sunlight.

Sunset was not far off. Dusk would come soon, and then the vast panorama of lights that the dead man had loved so well would flash from mammoth signs and marquees all along Broadway.

Hundreds of showfolk would return after a light supper to their dressing rooms to make up for a performance. On the Big Street the show must go on, but everywhere backstage, from the burlesque houses on Forty-second Street to Loew's State, the Casino, and the Palace, talk would center on the last, the greatest, the most brilliant, and yes, God damn it—the most *beloved* impresario of them all, who had left the scene too soon.

On Sunday, July 24, a *New York Times* story under the heading "Passing of Ziegfeld Saddens Broadway" told of a brief service held in a Hollywood chapel, and of Billie Burke Ziegfeld's intention to travel east with her husband's body after she had finished *Bill of Divorcement*.

In speaking of *Show Boat*'s Saturday matinée, the writer cautiously observed that "many must have been affected by the death of their exacting master." And also that it was a matter of general agreement among Ziegfeld's friends, including top-ranking rival producers, that his suddenly vacated, unique place in the American theater would never be filled, inasmuch as no one else could be expected to possess either his "instinctive taste and his passion for perfection" or that special "touch" that "nobody could define."

At some time during this sultry sabbath day, Mayor Jimmy

Walker telephoned Miss Burke, urging her to bring her husband's body east so that "the city in which he built his career might have an opportunity to honor him."

But Miss Burke gently refused, saying she was certain Flo wouldn't have wanted a public funeral.

The next day's newspapers were studded with further glittering tributes to Mr. Z, and the *Times* described the "simple services" at the Pierce Memorial Chapel in Hollywood to which "only 200 close friends" had been invited.

The dull silver casket, covered with a blanket of white and crimson roses, rested on a similar piece, surrounded by countless floral offerings from stage and screen stars. The luminaries who knelt for a few moments before the altar with Billie Burke and Patricia included Eddie Cantor, Marion Davies, William Randolph Hearst, Will Rogers, John Barrymore, Bebe Daniels, Ben Lyon, Harold Lloyd, and Mr. and Mrs. John Boles.

As to the effect Ziegfeld's death had on Helen Morgan, George Blackwood recalls that for a week she had spells, tipsy or sober, of sitting listless, staring directly ahead, and that she had trouble, offstage, in speaking above a whisper.

Ziegfeld, who in 1920 had mistakenly banished her to *Sally's* rear chorus line, had long since become a thoughtful, confidential friend, and Morgan may also have sensed that in his passing she had lost an irreplaceable, protective father figure.

11

Blackwood Moves In

GEORGE BLACKWOOD WAS LEARNING, in this trying summer of 1932, that the seemingly simple woman with whom he'd fallen in love was, in reality, a complex creature whose moods could vary from giggling schoolgirlish gaiety to a kind of morose sadness, surely caused by an ingrained insecurity dating from Tom Morgan's second defection—that final desertion after which the adolescent girl had felt compelled to look out for Lulu and "make things up to her."

Plainly, Helen was a mama's girl, and as the weeks passed George garnered increasing evidence that she had, paradoxically, a maternal sense of responsibility toward *Show Boat*'s cast and crew.

Except for George and her understudy, Miss Tierney, Morgan was not intimate with members of the cast. Nevertheless, her amazing compassion reached out to encompass not only her co-workers but members of their families in times of sickness or financial need.

On Broadway Morgan's reputation as a soft touch was common (and shameless) knowledge, but it was not generally known that she was as quick to give of *herself* to ailing friends as to fold greenbacks into the hands of old troopers who were "temporarily resting."

If someone in *Show Boat*, or even some kinsman of a player was hospitalized, Helen Morgan was the first visitor to appear with flowers and fruit. And if she was told to go to a ward, she refused to leave the hospital until the patient was moved to a private room at her expense.

At Bellevue, where most ailing and broke showpeople landed, the nurses and doctors had long since begun to joke about establishing a "Helen Morgan Wing" for the maintenance and special care of the lady's countless "cousins" who'd been mistakenly assigned to ward beds. Helen had once worked as a nurse, and now it seemed she couldn't live without doing whatever she could to cheer and comfort every ailing acquaintance.

In contrast to this Lady Bountiful program, her airy disregard of Blackwood's stealthy efforts to escape a nightly preperformance consumption of brandy seemed nothing short of capricious selfishness.

It was understood that George must share with her a few ponies of brandy before each performance, and his occasional ruse of arriving late at the theater, with just enough time to get into makeup and costume, proved unsuccessful.

On the few evenings when George tried sneaking in late, the lady's personal maid, Merandy, would stick her head in his door and cry, "Miss Helen say you better come on down, Mr. George. Say she already three shots ahead of you."

Then Blackwood would go down, ten minutes before curtain time, to find four ponies lined up for him on Helen's makeup shelf.

This was the way Helen wanted it, and George has said, "I swear, except a few times, when for some reason she chose to go on sober, I was always under the weather as Charles Winninger brought us on to introduce us as his *Cotton Blossom* leading lady and leading man. Helen just had to be fortified for that first entrance and the strange thing was, the few times she ever went on without brandy, her performance wasn't quite up to par. Brandy was the extra something she needed to effect that unique, all-embracing rapport with the audience which nobody, not even she, could altogether explain. I *know* this all sounds crazy, but it's a fact that she couldn't create that effect without a few shots of Old Three-Star Hennessy."

Actually, the explanation for this state of affairs may have

been simple. Being both reticent and shy, Morgan undoubtedly suffered, as countless super-sensitive performers do, from
an almost traumatic stage fright, not only at openings but in
the last half-hour before every performance during a run.
Somewhere back in this artist's mind there was always a secret
fear that perhaps *this* afternoon, *this* night, she'd be unable
to make the magic.

She had to be *with it* herself, singing "That Man" and
"Bill," in order to know she held them all, with a crystal final
note and a perfect gesture, cupped in her long-fingered hands.

It may have been, too, that Helen depended on prayer as
well as brandy to get her through trying dress rehearsals,
opening nights, and those rare times when, because of some
indisposition, she just didn't feel like going on.

Since childhood she'd seldom gone to bed without kneeling
down to pray, and though she belonged to no church, she was
at this time interested in the widely divergent faiths of Catholi-
cism and Christian Science.

While *Show Boat* was still in New York, George went with
her several times to the First Church of Christ Scientist on
Park Avenue, where she sat fascinated, not only with the
teachings of Mary Baker Eddy but by the performances of a
fellow actor, Felix Krems, who served as first reader on Sundays and sometimes as leader at Wednesday night testimonial
meetings.

Krems' mobile face seemed fixed in a cheek-lined, per-
petual smile from which Morgan's gaze seldom wandered—
except during moments when his toupée, always slightly
askew, threatened to slip. Often, too, she sat, breathlessly big-
eyed, marveling at some ardent Scientist's account of a miracu-
lous instant healing. Though she expressed no doubts regarding the testifiers' sincerity, she could hardly wait on such
nights to get outside and compare notes with actress Marjorie
Rambeau, another fervent faith-seeker, on the testifier's histri-
onic abilities.

Helen also loved to attend the Church of the Immaculate
Conception on Twenty-eighth Street (also known as the
Actors' Church and the Little Church Around the Corner),

where she met and chatted with thespian friends she might otherwise have lost track of. There on weekends in early autumn (residing by that time in a house with a front porch she'd bought in Brooklyn Heights)[1] she and Lulu and George attended mass at St. James Catholic Church on St. James Place.

For years she had been an avid fan of Los Angeles' Aimée Semple McPherson, whose performances at her famous Angelus Temple excited the awed admiration of such seasoned troopers as the Duncan sisters, who satirized her antics in their act—but Helen was never given to actual sacrilege. The ritual of the Catholic mass, especially at Christmas and Easter, held her spellbound. And even at this time, when she was not sure what faith she'd one day embrace, George noticed that she was enthralled by the candles, the incense, the gold and silver trappings, the gorgeous robes, the Latin incantations— and most of all by the congregation's rapt absorption in the rites of its religion.

Yes, where theology was concerned, Helen Morgan had never been able to probe or analyze, because faith had simply been instilled in her by Lulu and by her Episcopal Sunday school teacher in Chicago.

Emotional, even fatalistic by nature, this child-woman had need to embrace a creed based on the tenets of reward and punishment, of heaven and hell, of alternate guilt and remorse that must be expiated by confession, so that a personal God might be persuaded to grant His penitent servant divine forgiveness.

Morgan was intelligent, but it cannot be stressed too often that she was also sentimental, unsophisticated, and (for all her surface show of stoicism in grief) constantly tortured by fears of unrelenting reality and a possible early death.

By September of 1932 George Blackwood was ready to accept these and other contradictory manifestations of Helen

---

[1] She had also bought a farm near High Falls, New York, for Lulu's nostalgic pleasure.

Morgan's psyche. He knew that her fear of being left alone for long anywhere, any time, was real and uncontrollable.

Now, while the trees in Central Park turned brown and gold through days of mellow sunlight, she had moments of nostalgic, wistful sadness, but George was sure that in this season she was more often childishly gay and carefree with him than she'd ever been with most people, and he was willing to wait. For even though she avoided any serious discussion of their growing relationship, Blackwood was convinced that, Mr. Loew or no Mr. Loew, a time would come—and soon— when he could tell Helen Morgan that he was in love and expect to receive a like confession from her.

As it happened, George did not have to wait long—and surprisingly, it was Miss Morgan who took matters into her own hands, setting the stage for a change of scene.

When *Show Boat* closed after 192 performances on November 25, 1932, at the Casino, the big production took to the road, opening first at Ford's Theater in Baltimore where, on November 27, Paul Keath took over for Dennis King as Ravenal, William Kent replaced Charles Winninger as Cap'n Andy, and Bertha Belmore succeeded Edna May Oliver as Parthy Ann Hawks.

Using the old excuse, "You know I can never bear to be alone," Helen had instructed the show's advance man to reserve for her and Mr. Blackwood in Baltimore (and every other city) adjoining suites with connecting doors, and it was in Baltimore that George received a baffling surprise on the afternoon before opening night.

While he was at the theater for a special line-and-music cue rehearsal with three Jubilee Singers' replacements, Miss Morgan, who didn't have to be at the brief rehearsal, was rushing with Merandy from suite to suite at the Baltimore Hotel.

Arthur Loew had called her from the depot to say he'd come down for the opening at Ford's Theater, and by the time George got back to the hotel all *his* belongings had been whisked from the suite adjoining Helen's on the second floor to a single room on the third. Oddly enough, though, Loew was put into a suite on the fourth floor and the hastily cleared suite next to Helen's remained empty during his visit, so Blackwood was more than ever puzzled as to the relationship between Helen and Arthur.

Since Miss M didn't seem to care what the hotel management thought about Blackwood's being quartered indirectly with her, she'd obviously had him moved to allay any jealous suspicions in Arthur Loew's mind regarding her (thus far) innocent alliance with her leading man.

On the other hand, since Loew took a suite on the fourth floor, one could only conclude that either the lady or *that* gentleman was bending over backward to present a totally respectable façade in Baltimore. The whole thing was a mystery to George, and since Helen made no attempt to clear it up, he would remain forever in doubt as to the actions of Morgan and the man she so adored before Loew returned to New York the next day.

The company celebrated Thanksgiving in Baltimore, then moved on to open December 9 in Washington, D. C., where, to his not inconsiderable surprise, George literally moved in at the fashionable Haye-Adams House with Helen.

There, too, Blackwood was amused by a ritual he'd already observed in Baltimore. While he and Morgan registered, her maid Merandy was sent up ahead—as she would always be on this tour—to go over every inch of the bath and each door knob with Zonite.

This hygienic phobia (if it could be so designated) George would soon accept simply as an eccentricity such as is often encountered in an extremely fastidious person.

Merandy sent Morgan's stage costumes to the cleaners three times a week. They were picked up immediately after a final curtain call and returned just before the curtain rose on the next performance. Morgan had a special maid who cleaned and disinfected her dressing room twice a week, but even so, the sight of a cockroach once evoked screams that brought the stage manager at a gallop when the outburst reached the stage during a quiet love scene between Magnolia and Ravenal.

On tour Merandy, who had charge of her lady's fourteen pieces of cowhide and pigskin luggage, carried a tote bag of disinfectants, rags, sponges, brushes, and spray guns.

And while Helen and George waited in a hotel lobby, she scurried to the new suite to destroy whatever noxious germs former guests had left behind.

When she went up to the rooms that always smelled like a hospital, Helen invariably took out of her makeup case an atomizer filled with Chanel No. 5 and vigorously tried to dispel the clinical atmosphere.

At one stand on the tour her delicate skin broke out in a rash and she screamed at the maid, "Damn you, woman, you missed a spot in here."

Merandy, in righteous rebellion, yelled back, "You and your goddamn phobia. I bet you spray yourself all over every time you so much as kiss a man."

Morgan collapsed in helpless laughter, but there at the Haye-Adams House in Washington, as everywhere else, she and George waited in the lobby until Merandy's meticulous chores were completed. And after that a portable bar, generously stocked with expensive liquors, was always set up in the suite.

In Baltimore, when George remonstrated about her lavish stock, Helen answered, "Oh, darling, you know how embarrassing it is when a guest asks for something you haven't got and you have to send someone out for it."

As was the case with room sterilization, Morgan had to have her own extravagant way in this matter—and this night in Washington, George knew, her suite would be filled, as it had been in Baltimore, with a motley collection of characters including high-ranking politicians, chorus girls from the cast, society fans, discreetly tailored gangsters, call girls, and even pimps, all ready and eager to slake their thirsts at the lady's expense.

That night, however, after a brilliant formal dress opening, the general exodus to the Haye-Adams House was delayed, due to the unexpected presence backstage of a couple named Roosevelt who lived in a white house across the park. Eleanor was there with Franklin to toast one of the great stars of *Show Boat* with special sherry, fetched from the presidential mansion.

This was Blackwood's second surprise of the day. The third occurred when he entered his suite to find a pair of silk pajamas, a Sulka dressing gown, and leather slippers laid out, with instructions for him to change into this garb before he joined the party.

George did as he was told, and when he entered Morgan's living room he found her gorgeously attired in a floating hostess gown with a train, so there was no doubt in the Blackwood mind as to the lady's intentions.

In later years George could never remember whether it was on this night or the next that his affair with Helen was consummated, nor could he recall who, precisely, instigated the exodus from the living room to Helen's bedchamber, but he has said, with a reflective grin, "I *think* we just got up and wandered in there, hand in hand."

His recollection of the ensuing first-night events would always be a bit hazy, but he was to learn that even though the French attitude toward sex was no surprise to Miss Morgan, the various acts of love were always performed in total darkness.

Helen was no square between the sheets, but the only daughter of that straitlaced lady, Lulu, had no penchant whatsoever for such appurtenances as colored lights, Japanese aids, or mirrored ceilings.

On *Show Boat*'s second night in Washington, as Morgan left the National Theater accompanied by George, by the ex-clown Francis X. Mahoney, who played Rubber Face, and a few glorified chorines, she looked up at the bright moon and cried, "Oh, do let's walk. It's such a beautiful night, and our guests aren't due for an hour."

Her companions quickly agreed, so the entourage set out for the Haye-Adams House. And as they were strolling through Lafayette Park past some beds of red roses, Miss Morgan pausing to sniff the air, suggested, "George darling, why don't you pick a few of these lovely things for me? They'd look so lovely in our suite tonight."

George said, "Sure, why not?"

He managed, with Francis X. Mahoney's help, to gather a dozen beauties. Then, just as the party reached the entrance of the Haye-Adams House, Francis X. said, "George, old buddy, don't look now, but there's a squad car following us."

The star of *Show Boat* and all the chorines sped through the lobby to the elevator, and the two men followed at a jog-trot.

As Helen unlocked the door to the suite, the phone shrilled inside. She ran to answer it, then cried out, giggling and scared as she replaced the receiver, "The desk clerk says there's an officer on his way up."

Five minutes later a young, ruggedly handsome member of the capital city's police force was standing in the corridor door, enquiring, "Did you folks know there's a five-dollar fine for every rose picked in a Washington park?"

Miss Morgan's white hand flew to her breast as she answered in dulcet tones, "Oh, lieutenant, how on Earth could we have known? There's no sign anywhere. I really am terribly sorry, but mayn't we offer you a drink while we discuss this matter?"

By now Francis X. was behind the bar, busy with ice and glasses. The young cop, obviously mesmerized by the sight of Helen Morgan in the flesh, murmured something about "Well, thank you, maybe a little one," and even as he moved toward the bar, Francis X. set out a dark scotch and soda.

Mahoney's teeth flashed, bright as the two-carat diamond ring on his right hand, as he cried, "Here you are, captain," and the comely cop—twice promoted in less than fifteen minutes—accepted the offering with thanks.

Other guests were arriving now, and the officer's blue eyes danced as he watched the influx of capital bigwigs and famous showfolk. By the time he'd downed a second scotch, he seemed to have forgotten about the stolen roses, absorbed as he was in watching Miss Morgan's floating glide to the ringing telephone.

She said, "Hello? Oh, yes. And you say the officer's car is blocking traffic? Why, certainly. I'll ask him to come right down."

She hung up the receiver and moved to the bar, saying, "Francis X., wrap up a bottle of scotch for this nice man." Then she beamed at the cop and cooed, "Officer, I'm sorry you have to go, but when you're off duty, why don't you come back for a nightcap?"

The officer departed, bowing right and left, with the well-wrapped bottle under his arm, and the Morgan party went on.

At somewhere near three-thirty the last straggling guests departed, and as George turned from closing the corridor door he noted that Helen's eye and lip makeup had gone askew.

George moved to where she stood at a window that looked out on the White House. He touched her arm and spoke softly. "Honey, don't you think we should go to bed? One more brandy and those pretty knees of yours are just bound to buckle."

Miss Morgan's perfect nose ascended. She pushed back the draperies, crying, "Oh, my God, I'm beautiful"—and started crumpling.

George sprang forward, scooped her up, and staggered toward the bedroom, his progress somewhat hampered by a steady barrage of fist raps.

As he neared the bed, he lost his balance and fell on top of the lady. The two bodies struck the mattress, and the ancient bed's foot and head boards collapsed. The bombed-out pair lay prone in a mass of slats and springs; then, as they strove to emerge from the tangle of bedclothes, a passkey turned in the door's lock and a burly house detective entered, bellowing outrage.

He stopped yelling just long enough to summon Merandy by phone from her room in the hotel's maid quarters, then resumed his lecture on the proper behavior of guests in a house that had sheltered Washington's elite since the days of President Garfield.

Miss Morgan looked up, bleary-eyed, white cheeks streaked with mascara, and cried to him, in a thick voice, "Now, Mr. Detective, surely you're not going to throw us out just because of a silly accident. What else could you expect of a bed George and Martha slept in?"

By this time Merandy was struggling unsuccessfully to get her mistress into street attire, but the big house dick, outraged by the lady's belittling remark about the Haye-Adams' accommodations, now set up such a clamor of "Out, Out, I said," that the poor maid quickly draped Morgan's mink coat over her shoulders and began, with Blackwood's dubious assistance, a retreat toward the corridor.

The party of four finally reached the lobby; then Merandy sped back upstairs to pack trunks and valises.

The culprits were ushered onto the sidewalk just as day broke. Their baggage was presently trundled out, then the *Show Boat* publicity man appeared on the sidewalk, moaning, "Oh, my God, how awful! I only hope the press doesn't get hold of this. Now, listen. I've already called the Statler and the manager says he'll take you in, but you'll have to use the basement trade entrance."

He whistled for a cab, groaning as the driver drew up at the curb, "Thank God, it's too early for business traffic. Now, when you get to your rooms, someone will bring up a registration pad. Sign it, go to bed, and get some sleep. This is a matinée day, and you two have to be in your dressing rooms by two o'clock at the latest."

As George helped Helen into the cab, she sank into the seat, sobered and shaken. Then, as the cab driver broke into guffaws, the bedraggled pair in the back seat fell shrieking into each other's arms.

They were still young, and they had each other. It would take more than one night's misadventures with a cop and a house detective to quench their delight in being so much alive and in love.

12

Princess Helen

AFTER WASHINGTON *Show Boat* played Pittsburgh, Columbus, Cincinnati, and Cleveland, where on December 23 Blackwood telephoned his family at Canton, sixty miles away.

From Helen's suite at the Statler he spoke, in turn, with his parents, his sister, Hazel Marie, and her new husband, Donald Fulton, promising that he'd be with them on December 27 when the Hanna Theater would be dark.

Those were his plans, but the wily Miss Morgan, who'd jotted down the number he gave the operator, had some plans of her own. When he'd left the suite she, too, phoned Canton and made certain arrangements for the next day with George's parents and the Fultons.

Knowing so little about her own lineage, Helen had been fascinated by the facts George had gradually revealed about both sides of his family.

His mother, Myrtle Bell Hughes, a native of Wales and a niece of the painter John Singer Sargent, had met Frank Lee Blackwood on a visit to his family's farm in Lancaster, Pennsylvania, where they were later married. The couple settled down on their own farm near Dalton, Ohio, where Frank began to breed and trade horses, in partnership with William Gable of Cadiz, Ohio, whose husky, dark-eyed son William, Jr., would one day change his first name to Clark and finally be known—after playing Rhett Butler in *Gone with the Wind*—as the King of Hollywood.

Frank Blackwood, who had emigrated to Ohio from Ireland by way of London, was a member of the family who owned and published *Blackwood's Magazine* and he'd often been heard to say, "I'm just a dry twig off the literary branch, I guess, but I'm a damned good farmin' horse trader."

George and his sister had been born on the Dalton farm, and Hazel Marie, having studied piano and decided she'd never make it on the concert stage, had taken up china painting and married Donald Fulton, a virile, attractive young man who hailed from an Ohio hamlet called Canal Fulton.

Helen Morgan was eager to meet these people, especially the dark-haired Myrtle Bell, who was five-feet-nine, almost as good a cook as Lulu (according to George), and hopelessly stagestruck because of having once been voted, in a contest at Canton's Grand Opera House, "the most attractive woman in the state of Ohio."

So Helen told George, on the morning of Christmas Eve, that she planned to go shopping for his "Christmas" as well as for some last-minute gifts, then took off in a taxi for downtown Cleveland to secretly meet the members of his family, who were driving in from Canton.

Because of her careful planning, George was due for a fabulous surprise—and, as it happened, so was she because of a trip she'd asked him to make, after her return from downtown, to a nearby drugstore for a special stick of stage makeup.

On his way back to the hotel, in the late snowy afternoon, George suddenly bumped headlong into a man in circus regalia with a pale gold lion cub tucked under one arm.

The two men exchanged apologies and George said, "My, what a beautiful animal! Would it be all right if I touched it?"

The clown said, "Oh, sure, She's such a baby she doesn't even know about teeth and claws yet."

So George stroked the silky head, asking, "Does she belong to you?"

"No, not really," the clown said. "I'm with Evans Brothers Circus and she's part of the small menagerie we've rented out to the toy shop at Halle's department store. Besides this beauty,

I'm working with a baby chimp, a bear cub, and a little elephant, but I always take this one out to supper with me. She's still so gentle I'm afraid someone might be tempted to steal her."

George said, "I think you're right, there." Then, possessed of a sudden, wild impulse, he began, "Look, I'm playing with Helen Morgan, over at the Hanna Theater . . ."

The clown cut in, smiling. "I know. I caught the show last night, so I already recognized you, Mr. Blackwood. My name's Alan Stout."

The men shook hands. Then George said he wished it were possible for Miss Morgan to see the cub.

The clown's eyes twinkled brightly. "Okay. Let's make a deal. I'll let you borrow the baby if you'll introduce me to Helen Morgan when I come back for her after the show."

George said, "You've got a deal." The man passed the cub over, telling him to wrap her silver chain around his hand, and George trudged on through the sifting snow, attracting considerable attention from last-minute Christmas shoppers.

When he opened the door to Helen's suite, she sang out from her dressing table, "Well, well. Home at last, dear George. What ever took you so long?"

George didn't answer as he entered the bedroom. Then Morgan looked in the mirror, and quickly stood up, gasping.

"*George*, that is the *most* beautiful thing I've ever seen in my life. Where on Earth did you get it?"

George explained, and Helen kissed the cub on the head, pleading, "Then, since we can have her for just a few hours, let's not eat until after the show. We'll stay here and get acquainted with her. But first, let's give her some of that chicken in the bar icebox, darling."

They fed the cub and played with her for more than an hour, then took her with them to the Hanna Theater in a taxi.

As they entered Morgan's dressing room, Merandy let out a shriek and her mistress had a hard time persuading the maid to come anywhere near Baby. Various white cast members popped their heads in to ooh and ah, but when the Jubilee

Singers arrived most of them exhibited an utterly amazing reaction.

Recalling the scene, George Blackwood said, "What I'm saying is true, and I'll swear to it. As soon as they came in the stage door, those black people smelled the cat and stopped dead in their tracks, eyes and nostrils widened, reacting just like primitive Africans. They wouldn't go near Helen's dressing room, and during the bloodletting scene they stayed as far as possible from Steve and Julie. Damnedest thing I ever saw in my life, but anyone in that cast who is still alive can tell you it actually happened."

But if the Jubilee Singers were having no part of Baby, the chorus kids made up for their defection. They came in swarms to Morgan's dressing room, and when George ran downstairs before the first curtain he was pleased to find only half the usual quota of brandy ponies awaiting him.

After the show Alan Stout came back with one of the Evans brothers, who was also eager to meet Miss Morgan, and George introduced the men to her before he went up to change.

He took off his makeup, changed into street clothes, and came down again to find Helen standing by the stage door, talking to Evans and to Alan Stout, who had the cub in his arms.

From a distance George saw Morgan give Evans a piece of paper that he supposed she'd autographed. She said something to Stout, slipped a Statler room key into his hand and said good-night to the two men. Then she tripped over and asked George to thumbtack a note on the callboard that read:

> Children, don't come to our suite until midnight. Then all
> of you come together. Late stragglers won't be welcome.
> Merry Christmas and love from Julie and Steve.

On the way home to the Statler Helen refused to divulge any information about the cub or her conversation with the circus men, but when she stopped at a delicatessen to pur-

chase three pounds of rare roast beef and six cans of condensed milk, George decided she'd arranged with Evans to
keep Baby until after their party. True, she'd bought enough
food for six lion cubs—but then, Helen had never learned the
meaning of moderation in anything.

At the hotel she skipped out of the elevator on the sixth
floor, telling George, "Now, darling, there are two rooms on
this corridor in which you'll find the first part of your Christmas."

Stopping, she pushed a bell and the door swung open
revealing his family, en masse.

There was much kissing and handshaking; then George
stepped back to admire his womenfolk.

Myrtle Bell and Hazel Marie had on their first formal evening dresses, and his mother displayed a tag attached to her
person inscribed: "To Mother Blackwood, with my love—
Helen Morgan."

Myrtle Bell said proudly, "She took us on this marvelous
shopping spree and I made her write on this tag. I'm never
going to take it off as long as I live, so help me."

Everybody laughed, and then Helen led the parade down
the corridor, telling George that he mustn't go into his suite
until all the guests had arrived.

The living room of Miss Morgan's apartment was truly
something to see. She had bought gifts for everyone in the
Show Boat entourage, and as they finished assembling, she
made a quick exit into George's suite.

After a moment, she came out again with the lion cub,
placed her in Blackwood's arms, and cried, "Merry Christmas, George. This darling belongs to *us* now."

She asked Alan Campbell, a member of the *Show Boat*
cast who'd once been a real-life country preacher, to christen
the cub, and he sprinkled a few drops of water on the creature's golden head, intoning, "In the name of St. Francis of
Assisi, who watches over all animals, and with a prayer to the
good Lord to grant her a long, happy life, I christen this
lioness Princess Helen."

Everybody cheered. Then Francis X. Mahoney passed

around trays of champagne, and the ex-preacher cried, raising his glass. "Merry Christmas to Princess Helen and Julie and Steve."

After that, Helen served the Princess a grown lion's share of roast beef on a Statler plate and began, with Mahoney's help, to play Santa Claus.

George Blackwood looked on, marveling. This year he'd seen Morgan in action prior to the holiday season. In addition to shopping for Lulu and special friends in New York, she'd somehow managed to purchase gifts for the 120 people connected with the road company. And George would presently learn that she'd paid Evans three hundred dollars for the Princess, giving no thought to the problems that would most certainly arise as this wild creature matured.

Christmas to Helen Morgan (as has been noted) was truly a time for spreading good cheer, and the hell with stinginess. If she and Blackwood wanted this tawny playmate, why shouldn't they have her?

George sighed as he watched her dispensing largesse. Money would never mean anything to this woman except as a means of bringing solace, comfort, and maybe a small share of happiness to the people she cared about in this by no means best-of-all-possible-worlds.

In the first week of the new year, 1933, *Show Boat* reached Chicago where Helen and George checked into the small Eastgate Hotel next door to the studio of James Hargis Connelly, a fine photographer who, in a series of late night sessions, produced some excellent studies of his subjects—as Julie and Steve, and also as themselves.

The show stayed at the Oriental Theater for twelve weeks, then moved on to Indianapolis, Kansas City, Denver, St. Louis, Dallas, and, finally, before swinging back South, to Houston, Texas.

In Houston, toward the end of a brief run, an unforeseen problem was made manifest in a telegram from *Show Boat*'s publicity man.

The show had been booked to play all major cities throughout the South. Now it had become apparent that no town below the Mason-Dixon line could provide decent accommodations for the fifty black cast members. In the 1930s there were no hotels for Negroes in such cities as Mobile, New Orleans, Birmingham, Atlanta, Memphis, or Nashville, and the shack restaurants in segregated sections mainly served such rations as chitlins, hog jowl, blackeyed peas, grits, ham hocks, and catfish—all delectable dishes to Southern and even Harlem blacks but hardly suitable as a steady diet for singers.

Aware of this situation, a number of blacks had turned in their two-week notices before *Show Boat* left Houston. As soon as the Southern tour was cancelled by the general booking office, most of the Jubilee group decided to stay on with the company.

Thus, *Show Boat* packed up and headed east from Houston, forced by deplorable circumstances to forego enormous profits from intelligent Southern playgoers deprived of seeing the century's greatest breakthrough musical which dared to deal with miscegenation and backwoods bigotry.

Paul Robeson would soon bow out as Joe, to be replaced by Jules Bledsoe, not because of the Southern cancellations, but because of a second concert tour of Europe's capitals, where the color of an artist's skin was no deterrent to his being treated like any other decent citizen.

Now, playing the Eastern return circuit, Miss Morgan found herself carting along an extra valise crammed with books on the care and feeding of a captive jungle creature who was growing fast—in height, length, and weight.

She'd recently wired the advance man that she and George must be booked into hotels near public parks. He wired back, asking if Julie and Steve had taken up jogging, and she answered: "No, but our guest, the Princess, must spend much time with Mother Nature."

Intrigued, the advance man wired again: "What country is your princess from?" Helen gleefully answered: "Princess born in America but parents and forebears from darkest Africa."

As a result of these exchanges, she was surprised, at the next road stop, to find that she and George had been booked into a second-class hostelry smack on the borderline of an all-black neighborhood.

Show Boat veered west to play Los Angeles, San Francisco, Portland, and Seattle, then made a sleeper jump to Quebec before returning to the States for a two-week run at Detroit's Cass Theater.

On the day after the first night in Detroit, Helen asked George to take her out by trolley to the Bonstelle Playhouse on Woodward Avenue, where he'd played leads with the world-renowned Jessie Bonstelle. George was appalled to find only a ghost house desecrated by a group called the Wayne University Players.

Miss Jessie's goldleaf and mahogany paneling had vanished under a coat of dead white paint; her red velvet hangings had been replaced by burlap, and her crystal chandeliers, by bleak fluorescent tubes.

Standing under the fluorescent glare that drains the human countenance of any natural color, George's face grew even more ashen from nausea, and Helen told him, "Oh, darling, I'm sorry I suggested coming out here. I had no idea you'd find anything like this."

George said, "No. It's all right—except I have to get out in the air. Oh, God, Helen, why couldn't they have left her theater like it was—a beautiful place, full of heart-breaking memories?"

Helen reached out for his hand. "George, don't you know, when the moving spirit of a place like this is gone there's nothing left except a few worthless old bronze plaques?"

Depressed, the pair returned to the Tuller Hotel to exercise the Princess, who awaited them, restrained by a recently purchased steel-linked chain.

Starting with its last engagement in Chicago, the company had been playing a ravaged version of *Show Boat* that Blumenthal and Peggy Fears had instigated in the hope of raking in more shekels. There had been many cast changes, and

Helen Morgan was now the star of a truncated one-and-a-half-hour, thrice-a-day vaudeville revue with which the cast was disgusted.

Show Boat was no longer its beautiful self, and as if that were not enough, Helen and George had soon to face a parting with the Princess, who'd lately discovered the real purpose of teeth and claws.

Nothing was at all the way it had been at Christmas—and Helen Morgan, suffering periodic fits of depression, had been drinking far too much throughout this engagement at the Cass Theater.

After a fortnight in Detroit the company shuttled back to Cleveland, where problems arose in regard to the lioness. The Statler Hotel's manager insisted that she must not be left alone in the hotel. Then a polite young cop arrived at the Morgan suite with orders from headquarters that she couldn't be led through the downtown area, so Helen decided to rent a car.

One day, driving alone with the Princess, she ran through a red light, received a ticket and a warning, after arguing with the law, and just managed to reach the theater in time to make up for the daily grind. As a result of her altercation the theater manager arranged to have her represented in court by Maurice Mashke, Jr., son of Cleveland's Republican boss— and the young attorney's skillful pleading, which saved Helen undue publicity, also started a chain of events that would lead to a future consummation by no means devoutly to be wished.

Actually, Morgan had no more idea of getting romantic over this young man than she had of marrying George Blackwood, whose proposals she had gently refused three times, but a time would eventually come when, out of intense loneliness, she would listen to a proposition from Mr. Mashke.

Just now she was mostly concerned with increasing problems caused by the Princess's alarming growth, and when the Jubilee Singers planned a party in her honor at the New Orleans Club, she was thrown into a quandary by their request that she and George arrive unaccompanied by their rambunctious pet.

Helen was all for begging off from the party, but George decided that, rather than risk offending the Jubilee Singers, they might—just this once—disregard the hotel manager's edict and leave the lioness chained to a radiator valve.

Morgan said, "All right, we'll do that. Louis Armstrong's at the New Orleans Club, and I would love to hear him do 'When the Saints Go Marching In.' Right after that, maybe we can slip away without hurting anyone's feelings."

But this was, of course, merely wishful thinking. At the club, having finished his turn, Satchmo walked straight to Helen's table and begged her to beguile the crowd with "Bill."

Morgan said brightly, "Oh, Louis darling, I'd love to, but you're using a baby grand and I've always sung from an upright."

Satchmo grinned and told her, "Then, dear lady, we'll just get you an upright."

Two bus boys wheeled an upright piano onto the floor, and Helen, in great form, gave them "Bill" and "Can't Help Lovin' That Man," then got a laugh when she told the crowd, "I'd love to go on singing for you all night, but Mr. Blackwood and I must get back to the Statler. We have a lioness chained up there and the night maid may have already lost a leg."

Back at the hotel the two half-loaded revelers entered the Blackwood suite and there stood paralyzed, suddenly cold sober, as the Princess padded toward them, swinging her golden tail.

George had left her with too much chain, and she'd whiled away the nocturnal hours by tearing apart a pair of upholstered chairs.

Recalling the scene, Blackwood marvels, even now, at the animal's sterling performance. "She'd turned those chairs upside down and chewed right through the seat webbing. Those inner coil springs must have shot out like Roman candles on the Fourth of July. The chairs were entirely stripped of fabric, and most of the springs, twisted 'round the center chandelier, dripped strands of stuffing like Spanish moss from the limbs of a live oak tree."

When Morgan found her voice, she said, all in one breath, "Now, George, we mustn't be angry. She didn't know any better."

Blackwood sat down, scolding gently, "You're a bad, bad cat. Aren't you ashamed of yourself?"

The Princess turned her golden gaze on him; then, as George reached out to pat her head, she took his wrist in her mouth, as she'd often done, but this time she didn't let go. So George lowered himself into a sitting position while Helen besought him in a whisper not to move.

The lioness held on while she ran to the bar icebox for a bowl of dog food; then, as the creature released George's hand, Morgan spoke softly.

"I guess it won't matter now if we take her down in the freight elevator for a walk along some back streets. It may be for the last time, George."

On the walk, their charge behaved with docility until she reached an alley littered with discarded tin cans. Then, pulling George by her chain, she rolled the cans with her paws, tossed a few into the air, and raised a racket that caused her keepers to begin a hasty return trip, fearful of some alerted squad car's approach.

They made it safely back to the hotel, but the door to George's suite was standing open, and as they entered the front room the night manager, flanked by two maids, faced them.

"Miss Morgan," he said with restrained fury, "We have had, down the years, considerable experience with destruction in this hotel, but nothing, at any time, that could compare with *this*. Today I will have an upholsterer in for an estimate, and his price will be added to your bill. You people have until tomorrow afternoon to get this wild beast out of the Statler."

As the man left the suite, followed by the maids, who gave the Princess a wide berth, Helen ran to get a portfolio that contained, along with contracts and other papers, the telephone number of the Evans Circus's winter quarters at Massillon, Ohio.

It was now daylight, so she and George had breakfast and

waited, half dozing, until after eight o'clock, when she called the number, only to be told that the circus had gone on tour.

She hung up the receiver, saying, "Well, what now, I wonder?"

George suddenly sprang to his feet. "Give me the phone," he said. "I have an idea."

He called his home in Canton, explained the situation, and asked his mother to contact their friend the mayor in regard to presenting the lioness to Canton's Nimicella Park Zoo.

Myrtle Bell agreed to do what she could, and soon called back to report that the mayor had started the park's head zoo keeper toward Cleveland.

The man arrived with his truck that looked like a dog catcher's wagon, and the Princess's owners took her down, with her toys, in the freight elevator.

As soon as a brisk exchange of papers had been effected, the three people tried to coax the lioness into the truck's cagelike body, but she would have none of that.

In the end she was persuaded to occupy the front seat next to the driver and Helen and George stood tearful, watching the truck roll out of sight.

13

Hollywood Beckons
Blackwood

HELEN WEPT OFF AND ON, all day. And that night after the show, she said, "I can't stand going back to that hotel right now, George. Let's go out on the town."

They did the town, hitting most of the late spots, and stepped out of a taxi in front of the Statler, feeling no pain.

At the front desk the night clerk gave George his key and a telegram that he opened and read aloud:

> MRS. WARNER AND I SAW PERFORMANCE TONIGHT. BOTH FEEL YOU HAVE PICTURE POSSIBILITIES. IF THINGS CAN BE WORKED OUT WOULD LIKE TO HAVE YOU IN OUR ORGANIZATION. AM SENDING ON ARTHUR LANDAU, AN AGENT I LIKE TO DO BUSINESS WITH. HE WILL ARRIVE IN CLEVELAND NEXT FEW DAYS.—JACK WARNER

George looked at Helen, laughing. "Somebody in this crazy company's always playing tricks."

Morgan said, "Well, I don't know about that."

Upstairs, she called the Cleveland Hotel, asked if Jack Warner was registered there, and hung up, sighing, "He's there all right."

Two days later Arthur Landau, who represented such stars as Jean Harlow, Cary Grant, Carole Lombard, and Marie Dressler, arrived in town to watch an evening performance of *Show Boat*. Afterward, at the Statler, he discussed George's screen possibilities, his looks, a photographic resemblance to Gary Cooper, and the "Gable-esque quality" that Brooks Atkinson had once noted in a review.

Landau was ready to make up a representative's contract, and he must have Blackwood's decision pronto.

All through the agent's appraisal Helen had sat almost completely silent. Now George asked Landau to excuse him and Miss Morgan for a moment.

Once the door had closed, Helen said quickly, "You can't say no to this thing, George." Then she turned her back, speaking softly. "I've already lost one creature I loved this week. Now, if I lose you, too, it may be the end for me—but I still say you mustn't turn down this proposition."

George then said the usual things that lovers say, such as "You know you can never lose me, really," but Morgan's attitude seemed, as usual, fatalistic, and he was more than ever baffled by her "strangely submissive personality."

When he and Landau had signed the contract, which Helen witnessed, the agent called Hollywood and spoke to Jack Warner, who said he'd send on a Warner Brothers–First National contract at once, as well as a money order for George's train fare from Cleveland to Hollywood.

Then the big boss spoke directly to his new find, telling him that Warner's producer, Hal Wallis, planned to cast him with Kay Francis and Edward G. Robinson in a film called *Red Meat*, and finished by saying, "Tell that gorgeous Helen Morgan, as soon as she's free of your road tour, I'll have a script all ready for her consideration."

George thanked Warner, hung up, and repeated the message to Helen, who said absently, "That will be fine." Her face was smooth and oddly expressionless.

When Landau had gone, she made an obvious effort to seem optimistically cheerful, but George was not convinced by her performance.

These two had been extremely close, and no one knew better than Blackwood how much this reticent woman, who had no close friend other than himself in the company, except her maid, was already dreading the thought of being alone offstage for the rest of this tour.

Throughout the next two weeks, playing the daily vaudeville grind, George grew increasingly anxious on several counts about both himself and Morgan.

He was afraid that Helen might fall for her new Steve or, failing that, start drinking beyond all reason and become more reckless than usual about passing out hunks of her salary to chiselers.

All through the tour Blackwood had been concerned about her profligate generosity. Out of twenty-five hundred dollars a week, she sent four hundred to Lulu and three hundred to the Farmer's Trust Bank in New York, then—far too often—squandered the remaining eighteen hundred and borrowed ahead on her salary.

True, George had been unable to do anything about the problem personally, but Helen *had* been happy on this tour, before the current three-shows-a-day routine began. Now everything was changed, and George dreaded the day of his departure. He and this generous, lonely woman had had a good thing going. Now no one could predict what the rest of this year would be like—not only for Morgan but for him out there in Hollywood with no real friend to depend on.

When the New York casting agent Chamberlain Brown sent out to Cleveland an actor named Richard Sheridan to replace Blackwood as Steve, Miss Morgan ran through the bloodletting scene with the young man, thanked him, waited until he'd left the theater, then told the stage manager flatly, "I'm sorry, the boy won't do. He's too young and not even as tall as I am. I think we'd better give the part to the Drip."

The stage manager agreed, and immediately set up a run-through with Gladstone Waldrip, a personable fellow who had been understudying George. Someone, with humorous affection, had nicknamed him the Drip, and everyone liked him, but as it turned out, Miss Morgan's maid was not altogether convinced of his capabilities.

On the night of Blackwood's last performance in Cleveland, when he entered Morgan's dressing room and registered surprise at finding the makeup board devoid of brandy ponies, Merandy told him, "Miss Helen sufferin' from lover-losin' fever, and she ain't takin' one sip of brandy tonight. Her and me came down heah this afternoon to send out laundry 'n' cleanin' and I seen the stage manager rehearsin' that new Steve. Believe me, Mr. George, you ain't got nothin' at all to worry about."

Helen looked up in the mirror, laughing. "Now, Merandy, you just hush your mouth. I *want* George to worry about that Steve, so's he won't forget me when he's making love to all those gorgeous Hollywood stars."

George assured Helen there was no chance of his forgetting her, and after the curtain rose on the first scene of *Show Boat* he was once more reminded (if indeed a reminder was necessary) that Morgan the memorable had once again contrived, with the help of her co-workers, an unforgettable gesture.

As usual, when Cap'n Andy introduced the *Cotton Blossom*'s leading lady and leading man, Helen crossed stage right to be surrounded by sixteen beaux and George came down stage left to be encircled by sixteen belles—but tonight he looked down in the pit and saw that all the orchestra men, sporting white carnation boutonnieres, were on their feet. The sixteen belles stood with their hands behind them; then, at a time signal in the musical score, their hands came forward, clutching nosegays with which they pelted Steve until he stood in a rainbow of fallen flowers.

In his dressing room, changing after the show, George thought he'd never heard so much scuffling about backstage.

When he emerged with his luggage, the stairs were lined on either side with the Jubilee Singers, the principals, the beaux and belles, the musicians, the cast and crew, all shouting good wishes. Then, as he made his misty-eyed way down, shaking hands, he saw Helen, his parents, his sister, an uncle, and an aunt, all waiting below.

As he reached the last step, Morgan held out a sealed envelope and told him, "George dear, you must promise not to open this till after the train pulls out of the station. Also, when you get aboard, walk straight through the cars to the observation platform."

Piling into a taxi with his parents, Helen, Hazel Marie, and her Donald, Blackwood noticed two buses lined up at the curb before the theater.

At the station he and Helen and all his family went through the gates onto the lower platform, and George kissed everyone. Then he swung up into his Pullman car and began walking—as he'd been told to do—toward the open-air observation platform on the last car of the train. Passing the club car's windows, he saw the Jubilee Singers lined up along the platform; then, as he stepped outside and the train began to move, they broke into "Ol' Man River."

George smiled and waved as the train gathered speed, and the singing kept right on as he leaned out, waving as long as he could see his family and friends, waving back from the platform.

When they were clean out of sight, he made his way to his compartment, sat down, and blew his nose. He took Helen's letter out of his pocket, opened the envelope, and found five hundred-dollar bills inside. The words of the letter danced before his wet gaze as he read slowly:

> Darling George, this is not a loan. Please accept it as a token of my love. I know the people at Warner's have made a reservation for you at the Knickerbocker, but that's no place for a rising young star to stay. I want you to go to the Beverly Hills Hotel and take a suite.
>
> I love you and will miss you more than I can say. Playing the bloodletting scene will be an ordeal, but I'll just have to close my eyes and imagine it's you there at my side.
>
> When the show closes, I'm going to stop over, on my way to New York, to spend a few days with your dear family, and visit the Princess, in Canton.
>
> Wishing you a good journey, and with all my love,
>
> Helen

George sat unmoving, holding the letter. His eyes and face were wet and he told himself, "I'm crying and I don't care."

He put the letter and the bills in the envelope, and stuck the envelope back in his inside jacket pocket.

There was a bottle in one of his bags that stood on the luggage rack, and he meant to break it out, right now.

As *Show Boat* ground out its last week at Loew's State in Cleveland, Morgan went stoically onstage to play the bloodletting scene beside the new Steve, with whom she had no special rapport.

The once triumphant production, trimmed to the tacky dimensions of vaudeville "tab," then moved on to Chicago's Oriental Theater where—to the unconcealed relief of a disgruntled company—the travesty closed on February 23.

All the cast except the star boarded a New York Central train for New York. Morgan took a Pennsylvania Railroad train to Canton, Ohio, where Myrtle Bell Blackwood, surrounded by some church cronies and her Dalton quilting bee, met the distinguished visitor at the depot.

Helen kissed Mother Blackwood, accepted a bouquet of garden flowers, and told the ladies, "This is the greatest trackside reception I've ever had in my life."

Next day she and all the Blackwoods celebrated Myrtle Bell's birthday, but the rest of her visit was saddened by news that had already reached George in Hollywood.

From her first day at Nimicella Park Zoo, the lioness had pined in confinement—refusing to eat in her usual lusty fashion, pacing up and down in her cage like a distracted child. She had died one afternoon while Myrtle Bell and Hazel Marie were with her, and a local veterinarian who had fought to save her believed that she had perished of malnutrition, fear of captivity, and downright homesickness for her two human friends, who had themselves been so depressed a fortnight past, after the zoo keeper's truck had borne her away.

Now, on the second morning of Helen's visit, she and Myrtle Bell gathered wild flowers and walked down behind the house to the animal cemetery where George's father had buried the lioness alongside several departed family pets.

Helen gazed at the bronze plaque Papa Blackwood had placed in the big, centered boulder of his cemetery plot and tearfully read his inscription:

> Rest lightly on them, O Mother Earth, who have trod lightly on thee.

Then she and Myrtle Bell placed their floral offering on the Princess's grave and walked slowly back to the house.

On the day of Helen's departure Myrtle Bell waited with her beside the Pennsylvania tracks for the Manhattan Limited, and Morgan told her in a forlorn little voice, "You know, Mother Blackwood, I really feel a little scared about going back East now that Mr. Ziegfeld's dead and George is in Hollywood."

Nevertheless, she was returning to her pleasant house in Brooklyn Heights, and Lulu, as always, would be there to welcome her, so her spirits must have risen as the train approached New York.

At home, she and Lulu talked for hours about personal matters, then Helen conferred with her agent in regard to possible nightclub or theater engagements.

Benton had nothing outstanding for her at the moment, and since neither he nor she would consider offers received during the last grind weeks of *Show Boat* from the gang-controlled small dives of Greenwich Village, Helen talked with her mother about taking a European vacation trip alone.

Lulu said, "Why of course, honey. Go abroad, by all means. While you're gone I'll run up to High Falls and see about raising some turkeys on that rocky good-for-nothing farmland."

Helen laughed and told her, "Seems to me I've been more involved with 'turkeys' than anyone else in show biz, but you may have something there. It's a cinch we'll never be able to harvest a crop of anything else on that place except flowers and weeds. Besides, looking after a flock of turkey chicks ought to keep you busy enough not to get too lonesome while I'm gone."

So Miss Morgan sailed on the liner *Paris* on March 25, telling reporters she planned to spend some weeks abroad "visiting friends"—but failing to mention to them (as she had failed to mention to Lulu) that one very special friend would be joining her on the Continent at a prearranged meeting place.

She stayed in Europe a little more than three weeks. Then, homeward bound one day toward the end of April, she walked up the *Conte Di Savoia*'s gangplank wearing a Paris frock, smiling, and quite alone.

On this return voyage she must certainly have been hounded by autograph-seekers and badgered by some ship official to perform on the liner's last night out, but there is no reason to assume that the handsome, dark-haired man who strolled the decks with her was generally recognized.

Apparently the couple had eluded the press in France, but a *New York Times* sleuth was right on hand when the ship docked in Manhattan to report on May 1, 1933, "Among the passengers who arrived yesterday on the Italian liner *Conte Di Savoia*, was Helen Morgan, actress and singer who has been abroad several months. [This was, of course, inaccurate.] Another passenger was Arthur Loew of Metro Goldwyn Mayer. Neither was named in the official passenger list."

This news man, disappointed because he'd obtained no quotable statement from Helen, was gratified to receive, in answer to the pointblank question, "Are you and Miss Morgan married," a resigned reply from Mr. Loew: "This report occurs about every other month and I presume it's about time for it to appear again. Miss Morgan and I are not married."

It would soon be apparent that this holiday interlude had seen the end of something, for now—surely on the rebound from the loss of George and a breakup with Arthur Loew—Miss Morgan indulged in a drastic, wholly unfortunate escapade.

14

Marriage to Mashke

UNKNOWN TO THE PRESS, on the morning of May 15, Helen and the Cleveland attorney Maurice Mashke, Jr., persuaded a prothonotary in New Castle, Pennsylvania, to open his office early and sell them a license with which to drive out to the Union Township office of Harris M. Reynolds, a justice of the peace, who joined them in bonds of supposedly holy wedlock.

This news finally reached the papers on July 17, and from that date to summer's end the private and public doings of Mr. and Mrs. Maurice Mashke, Jr., were screened by the haze of a period in which Helen Morgan, as far as the press was concerned, literally dropped from sight.

Less than two years later she would claim that she and her groom never really got to know each other, and apparently this odd pair did live together for only a few months, or maybe weeks, as man and wife.

Young Mashke worked with his Republican boss parent out in Cleveland, so it would appear that Helen never, in a sense, left home, though the truth about where she stayed most of the summer is anybody's guess.

On August 3, in the Los Angeles *Examiner*, columnist Harriet Parsons, only daughter of the Gay Illiterate, Louella, wrote that Helen Morgan, who had scored in *Applause*, would soon be coming out to the Coast to test for Dumas's *Camille* and maybe to star in a *Sweet Adeline* revival with

George Blackwood, who would also soon be making a screen test for the male lead role opposite Garbo in *Romance*.

Toward the end of August Helen did entrain for the Coast, and one bright morning Jack Warner summoned George Blackwood to the holy of holies. The lady was scheduled to arrive that afternoon, and George was delegated to drive into Los Angeles with a publicity man to meet her at the railroad station.

At the appointed hour he and the publicity man stood waiting at the station gate, along with some press people, but when the Super Chief pulled in Miss Morgan wasn't on it.

The publicist drove George back to Beverly Hills, and he'd just settled down in his living room with a long drink when Warner phoned to say Helen had called from Albuquerque, New Mexico.

Getting off there to stretch her limbs, she'd become intrigued by a squaw selling blankets who also was nursing a sick baby, and so had failed to hear the train conductor crying, "All aboard." She'd now be arriving on the shuttle train at Pasadena at 10 P.M., so Warner would like George to drive out there with the same publicity man.

This time La Morgan made it, Indian blanket, beads, and all, stepping blithely down from the coach to answer reporters' questions and pose, smiling, with Mr. Blackwood as a few flashbulbs exploded.

On the drive with George from the Pasadena terminal to Warner's, Helen rattled away about the plight of the American Indian. "You know, that squaw back there can't get her baby into a white doctor's office? Those old medicine men just stick a few more feathers into their hair, bang out a few extra beats on the tom-toms and beseech the Great Spirit for a miracle."

Later, in her suite at the Beverly Wilshire, she had a drink with George and told him that she was now a properly married lady, explaining, "After you left, Buddy Mashke followed me to Chicago. Then he came to New York this spring, after I got back from Europe, and one night we drove up to New

Castle, Pennsylvania, after visiting a few nightspots on the
way, and ended up next morning getting hitched."

No mention was made of Mr. Blackwood's previous proposals of marriage, which she'd refused, nor did she discuss
the ending, amiable or otherwise, of her long-time relationship with Arthur Loew except to say that on the *Conte Di
Savoia*, returning from Europe, he'd asked her to "Give up
nightclub engagements, thereby avoiding contact with the
types of men who operated them, and with the heavy-drinking
café society crowd."

George couldn't understand the marriage to Mashke, but
he was certain that she was now finished, romantically, with
him, and maybe with the MGM mogul.

Because he and she were both busy, George did not see
Helen again during her ten-day stay in Hollywood, but he did
hear from his agent, Arthur Landau, of Morgan's having suggested to the casting office at Universal that he be interviewed
about playing Steve in the forthcoming movie production of
Show Boat. Unfortunately, Jack Warner was asking $500 a
week on any farm-out deal for Blackwood, so Donald Cook,
a stock contract player at Universal who was earning $250 a
week, would end up opposite Morgan in that splendid cinema
success.

George made his test at MGM for *Romance*, charmed by
Greta Garbo, who told the technical director, Douglas
Shearer, "Don't bother about me, Doug. This is Mr. Blackwood's test, so just keep your camera fixed on him." Nevertheless, (again because of Warner's loan-out price), George
would finally lose the part to Gavin Gordon.

Indirectly he heard that Helen's test for *Camille* had been
fine, but nothing further appeared in the columns about that
or a *Sweet Adeline* revival, so these two were destined never
to work together again.

On Sunday, November 5, 1933, as Helen Morgan debuted
over the Blue Network's Station WABC in a new song program series, Texas Guinan lay dying in a British Columbia
hospital.

The two women had been close friends back in 1928 before Morgan quit the nightclub business, but Helen may not have heard the whole unsavory truth about Tex's final abrupt disappearance from the Broadway scene.

In 1931, having somehow got on the wrong side of the vicious mobster, Dutch Schultz, who swore she'd never again in his lifetime hostess a New York club, Guinan had pulled up stakes and hightailed it out of the United States.

She'd sailed on the liner *Paris* with her girls to open a "sucker" hotspot in the Gallic capital, only to be waylaid at Cherbourg by outraged officials of France's Labor Ministry, who confined her with *les jeune filles* to a hotel under "house arrest" until the date of the *Paris*'s return trip to America.

Undaunted, hellbent as ever to make hay with onerous publicity, the Queen lost no time in organizing a revue called *Too Hot for Paris*, which toured the States for almost two years, then disbanded in late October 1933 when she entered a Vancouver hospital with an intestinal infection that was to take her life.

Ironically, even as plans were being made for her one-time friendly rival's funeral, Helen's agent was negotiating for his client to begin an extensive engagement at the Simplon Club (formerly the European Club, at 26 West Fifty-third Street, run by Nick Prounis and Pete Kledauris). And strangely enough, since Helen's and Texas's paths had separated, it was not she but another nightclub hostess, the Kansas-born, international adventuress Belle Livingston, who received a plaintive SOS call from a baffled mortician.

It seemed that during the embalming process Miss Guinan's chins, tucked up by a few face lifts, had loosed their moorings, thus presenting an unprecedented problem to Campbell's erstwhile undaunted technician.

Belle took a long, speculative look at the corpse, then dispatched a courier for yards of pastel tulle in which to swathe the brass-blonde head and the artfully madeup face of her old, kind friend.

As for Helen's reaction to Guinan's passing, it is safe to assume, because of her mistaken assumption that Campbell's

was owned by the major's family, she did not join the stream
of fanatics who, all through the night of November 11, filed
past the bier where Texas lay in state. Certainly she was not
one of the seventy-five hundred persons who stood outside
the packed Campbell's chapel, unable to witness the Catholic
service or to hear the eulogizing newspaper columnist, Hey-
wood Broun, say, with obvious sincerity, "We who loved
Texas so much will keep her memory in our hearts and minds,
and that will be part of her immortality."

No, Miss Morgan would never have gone anywhere near a
funeral parlor owned by anyone named Campbell, but it's possible that she did stand on Fifth Avenue, watching the funeral
cortege in which big-name gangsters, doubly protected by
bodyguards whose cars whipped in and out of the Guinan
procession, were driven in armored limousines to a Long
Island cemetery.

Out there all hell broke loose as two thousand subhumans
burst through a barricade of twelve Manhattan cops and
brawny state troopers to strip the receiving vault of mums
and orchids and tear apart the blanket of roses that covered
the casket.

This shameless, obscene demonstration, which would have
thrilled Texas Guinan, was precisely the sort of sendoff that
never intrigued Helen. Still, it must have struck her as passing
strange that now, in November 1933, even as the queen of
New York's nightclubs was being interred along with Prohibition, she, Helen Morgan—who had sworn never to enter
that world again—was about to open, with a weekly salary of
twenty-five hundred dollars, at Nick Prounis's Simplon, in the
Shoemaker family's former townhouse.

A monstrous era had ended with Guinan's demise, and
here was Morgan, torchbearer to that era, starting afresh in a
new period of "respectable drinking"—at the very top of the
heap.

15

Going the Nightclub and Hollywood Route

In the entrance hall of the old Shoemaker mansion on Morgan's opening night, letters and telegrams of good wishes waited, piled high on the library table that flanked the staircase.

At six o'clock a balding, fat attendant swung open the iron-grilled street door, and the lady herself, murmuring good evening, walked past him in her mink coat, climbed the stairs and made straight for the second floor's tiny bar where she perched on a stool and ordered herself some brandy.

She sat there alone, self-conscious, pretending not to notice a dark-haired, very young man having his dinner at a nearby table, who couldn't keep his admiring eyes to himself.

After about ten minutes, when the bartender went out through the swingdoor to the kitchen, the young man suddenly rose, approached the bar, and said in a breathless rush, "Miss Morgan, I'm just one of the hired help here, but I feel I have to say, 'Welcome to the Club.' "

Helen spun about on the bar stool. Then, as the young upstart held out his hand, she covered it with both her own and said, "Oh, how *darling* of you. Thank you, so *very* much."

Shaken, yet ecstatic, the young man bowed his way out of the bar and walked fast toward the stairs. Within the Simplon's environs, as a maverick hireling being paid ten dollars a week plus two lifesaving meals a day to collect past-due bills, he had no right to say, actually, "I'm Gilbert Maxwell, a poet who's about to publish his first book, and one of your greatest admirers." But that didn't matter much. Helen Morgan was not Percy B. Shelley, but she was the idol of his small-town adolescence; he'd "seen her plain," she'd turned and spoken to him, and that was a wondrous thing to treasure always.

It did not occur to him, as he sped down the stairs and out past the balding doorman into the dusk-filled street, that his small gesture of courtesy might have been of some comfort to the beautiful woman drinking alone at the bar.

He had no way of knowing that Helen Morgan was suffering her usual pre-opening night tremors, but he would remember all his life the instant radiance that had changed her face as, clasping his hand, she'd said in her lovely voice, "Thank you, so *very* much."

Within three weeks after Morgan's arrival, the Simplon's evening business tripled.

Then came a day at dusk when the hatcheck girl was heard complaining, "Oh, Lord, what a headache that man Prounis has given me. Yelling and complaining all afternoon. And why? Because Helen Morgan asked for another five hundred dollars a week and got it."

Sometimes the club's help would be treated to Morgan's sessions with the orchestra, and the poet-bill collector would retain an enchanting glimpse of her on a sunny afternoon, as smiling, head uplifted, she lounged on the Steinway, throatily crooning, "Lazy Summer Day."

At show time, when the lights in the club dimmed out and the "spot" revealed Morgan in black velvet with the real pearls and her scarlet kerchief, there was no conversation, no passing to and fro of waiters, no clink of silver or china.

Whenever the lady sang now there must be no sound in the room except the lilting rise and fall of her voice.

On one occasion only, during a second show when a drunken party failed to obey this edict, the lady slid off the Steinway and floated away to her dressing room—from whence she did not return to finish a show that was costing Nicholas Prounis $250.

There was only one Helen Morgan. She gave from the heart, and patrons must listen in sympathetic silence, working *with* her (never against her) to help create the fragile spell of gentle melancholy that had become her trademark.

Christmas came, and everyone employed at the Simplon Club was remembered by Morgan. The hatcheck girl and the female restroom attendant received distinctive presents. The men were given handsome neckties with labels inside that said "Merry Christmas—Helen Morgan."

The lady was in the money and feeling chipper again. Those wretched last weeks of *Show Boat* and the weeks in Europe during which she'd lost the Princess, George Blackwood, and Arthur Loew were all part of the past.

As for the present's problems, Helen was, as usual, keeping her secret self to herself. Still, the hatcheck girl wondered aloud why Miss Morgan so often left the club alone. She was said to be married to a lawyer named Mashke, but where had he been since her opening in early November? Somebody said he'd been seen at the bar one night, but the hatcheck girl couldn't swear that was true. Anyway, why wasn't he around more often? What kind of marriage was this?

Helen stayed at the Simplon well into the winter of 1934, when she left for the Coast with a play called *Memory* by Myron C. Fagin that premiered at Los Angeles's Biltmore Theater and got the ax from a nameless Hollywood critic whose review appeared in the L.A. *Times* on May 11.

This was a drama about a "beautiful and seductive musical comedy star," christened Memory by her father after her mother had died giving birth to her. The plot dealt with the star's campaign to rekindle a talented playwright-lyricist-composer's creative fires, with the couple's affair, and with Memory's response, during the writer's divorce proceedings, to a plea from his son that she send his dad back home to his heartbroken mama.

Anyone who'd been in *Show Boat* in 1927 could have spotted a surface resemblance to the Morgan-Hammerstein "affair" (or nonaffair), as in *Sweet Adeline,* but in this opus Morgan was working without the sure-fire team of Jerry and Oscar.

The Los Angeles critic found the play "very drippy, very noble, very sad." Helen's performance must have stayed his scornful pen on her behalf, but she had cause to be depressed by his statement that "the extraordinary acting of young Master Jackie Searle," in his single scene as the son, transcended the playwright's "oversentimental and heavy-handed writing." For here, once again, was proof of Miss Morgan's contention that, no matter how fond an actress might privately be of dogs and kids, she should never get mixed up with such natural scene-stealers on stage or screen.

Having avoided this hazard in making three recent films, she fared better at the hands of motion picture reviewers in New York.

In *You Belong to Me,* another "backstage" movie for Paramount at Astoria, she was credited with rendering a "good blues number." In *Marie Galante,* a Fox spy film starring Spencer Tracy, made before she left Hollywood that year, she would be praised, along with Ned Sparks and Stepin Fetchit, for providing "amusing sketches" in a Panama café sequence.

This picture played New York's Mayfair Theater in November, when Helen must have been making *You Belong to Me* at Astoria, so she undoubtedly spent Christmas with Lulu, in Brooklyn Heights or at the farm near High Falls, New York, but she was certainly back in Hollywood in the early winter of 1935, working as herself in *Sweet Music,* with Anne Dvorak and Rudy Vallee.

All these films were potboilers, and Helen must have sat submissive on various sets, yawning now and again back of her scarlet kerchief as she awaited her turn before the cameras.

Even though she was seeing such old-time good friends as Irene Dunne and Cesar Romero, there is evidence that she must have found Hollywood dull in April when she made surprising headlines by suing for divorce, charging that Mashke had "forced her to work to support herself, called her uncomplimentary names and caused many embarrassing scenes." Then she added, somewhat contradictorily, "He's a fine boy, but he has to be in Cleveland and I have to be everywhere. You can't have a marriage on that basis."

Lately she'd been working in *Go into Your Dance,* a First National film featuring Al Jolson and Ruby Keeler, in which she'd be praised for her poignant rendition of a sad ballad, "The Little Things You Used to Do," but this was certainly not enough.

She was on a treadmill now, doomed to being cast as herself, or as a prototype of herself, in mediocre backstage musicals.

The pattern had, of course, been set with *Show Boat* and *Sweet Adeline,* but she'd been born to play Julie, and the role of Adeline, with its special material, had been designed to make the most of her distinctive qualities.

On the screen she'd been given no chance, aside from the great burlesque part in *Applause,* to prove her worth as a fine dramatic actress.

Nothing had come of the test she'd made for Dumas's *Camille,* so no one would ever know, given that "strangely submissive personality," those luminous hazel eyes, and that white, waxen skin—truly like a camellia flower—what magic she might have wrought in creating the role of the little doomed French cocotte.

Now in a bad, blue season, maddened as she must have been by a shabby situation she had no power to change, she grew uncharacteristically peevish, changing her attitude toward Mashke, in a deposition read on July 19 in a Los Angeles courtroom.

True, the wording of this paper sounds more like a pedantic lawyer's lingo than Helen's own, but one still detects a surprisingly vehement, even vindictive approach to the problem of "getting out":

> My money, which I earned, was used to pay all our living expenses. He never worked, nor did he ever try to find work. When I was talking to someone else, he had a habit of putting his hand under my arm in what appeared to be an affection-

ate gesture. In reality, he was digging his fingernails into my
tender flesh.

The deposition went on to say that Maurice "at one time"
wouldn't let his wife so much as speak to Oscar Hammerstein II, "in whose shows she hoped to appear"—a statement
that suggests Helen may never have quite tossed away a torch
from which sparks were evident to a jealous husband's eye.

Also, the claim that Mashke "never worked or tried to find
work" seemed to contradict Morgan's former claim that she
was seeking legal separation because of this "nice boy's
[having] to be in Cleveland" while she had "to be everywhere."

Actually, since Republican boss Mashke's offices were in
Cleveland, and Junior had to be there, then Junior must have
been working at least part of the time for Senior.

All in all the situation seems obvious. Helen wanted out
and Maurice, who didn't contest her charges, seems to have
been glad to get out, too, even at the cost of being branded a
parasitic, jealous spouse who surreptitiously dug his nails into
his better half's "tender flesh."

After the divorce Helen returned to Brooklyn Heights, and
to the House of Morgan, where she presided throughout the
summer and most of the fall.

She went once more to the West Coast, before the year's
end, to play Julie in the second movie version of *Show Boat*,
—and while she was gone, the last nightclub to bear her name,
unable to exist without her, declared bankruptcy.

The new *Show Boat* film opened at Radio City Music Hall
on May 14, 1936, and once again all the critics acclaimed
the Ferber-Kern-Hammerstein classic.

Produced by Carl Laemmle, Jr., under the direction of
James Whale, the picture featured Helen Morgan, Paul Robe-
son, Irene Dunne, Allan Jones, Charles Winninger, Helen
Westley, Queenie Smith, and Francis X. Mahoney.

The entire Universal production—including the new screen
transcription, all the players, and, of course, the score—was
acclaimed, with extra praise for Robeson's new song "Ah Still

Suits Me" and another new number, "Gallivantin' Around," which Miss Dunne sang as Magnolia.

In the *New York Times* Frank Nugent said that nobody could ever get enough of Paul Robeson and "Ol' Man River," adding that one could mention "with scarcely less enthusiasm" Miss Morgan's rendition of "Can't Help Lovin' That Man" and "My Bill," as well as the Dunne-Jones duets, "You Are Love" and "Only Make Believe," plus a brand new Kern-Hammerstein special for Jones. "I Have the Room Above Her."

Nugent found Miss Dunne "splendid" as Magnolia, and Allan Jones, as Ravenal, "equally well cast and in fine voice."

Through some oversight he did not mention Donald Cook, but since Cook never gave a bad performance in his life one may conclude that Miss Morgan found him satisfactory as her Steve.

Now that *Show Boat* was "in port again," this critic hoped it would "find safe harbor"—and, of course, this film version did make it, memorably and money-wise. There would be cause for rejoicing wherever it was shown, except for one sad circumstance: This was the last time anyone would see and hear Helen Morgan making her special magic as Julie.

Show Boat would not be remade during her lifetime, and no other Julie, on stage or screen, would break the hearts of an audience.

Furthermore (precisely as though in leaving *Show Boat* behind her she'd been jinxed) Helen now faced a future road that would run all the way downhill.

If she'd been available, she might have been starred—because of her former appearances in George White's *Scandals* —in the 1935 edition that opened at the New Amsterdam on Christmas Day.

She began rehearsing for the road production in the spring of 1936, and the show opened in Chicago on June 28 (with Willie and Eugene Howard as her co-stars), running until late September.

After that the *Scandals* made money for two weeks in 'Frisco, then moved on to Los Angeles, where the show closed, in the late fall, after playing to substantial houses.

16

The Road Downhill

WHEN HELEN CAME EAST again she returned either to the house in Brooklyn Heights or to the farm, where Lulu was now raising turkeys.

She was apparently neither working nor making news from January through October 1937, but in that month a *Times* reporter made what he could of her part in a motor accident —which proved that (work or no work), Miss M was living it up on the morning she set out with her secretary, Florence Rintoul, for a drive into South Brooklyn, with her chauffeur, William Gage, behind the wheel.

Her Cadillac collided at Flatbush Avenue and Plaza Street with another car driven by one John Fink, and Helen wound up with a left elbow contusion.

The secretary suffered lacerations of nose, ear, and cheek, and a Methodist Episcopal Service ambulance surgeon noted in his report that Miss Rintoul resided with Miss Morgan in Brooklyn Heights at 466 East 18th Street.

Gage, the chauffeur, young Fink, and Miss Rintoul revealed their ages. Miss Morgan refused to give hers and, after emergency treatment, she and her secretary climbed back into her car to be driven home by Gage, who hadn't so much as been scratched.

Nothing about a court action resulting from this collision appeared in the papers, but the *Times* soon noted that Helen was scheduled to face charges, at Actors Equity, of appearing in an "unauthorized benefit."

She was exonerated at an Equity meeting after pleading that she was told the benefit *had* been approved, and this tidbit also was recorded in the *Times*.

The use of such items as these—strictly small-time stuff—indicated that the gentlemen of the fourth estate were eager to make publicity out of anything that happened to an amiable actress-singer whose star seemed momentarily descendant.

Actually that star had entered a period of eclipse that would last until a day in 1941 when Miss Morgan was destined to make headlines that many a reporter friend, bolstered by booze, would bang out with reluctant fingers.

Throughout 1938 Morgan was not in the theater. She made no films, and if she appeared at any big club in New York that fact was not recorded in the metropolitan press. She was undoubtedly restive, dissatisfied, and (despite Lulu's fearful remonstrances) relying on booze to help her get through a period of financial anxiety.

In the following year she set out on a tour of the Loew vaudeville circuit, at a salary of twenty-five hundred dollars a week, even though she was by now existing chiefly on brandy.

In the spring, playing Atlanta, she found temporary companionship and protection in the person of Don Prince, an old friend connected with Universal pictures, who looked after her as best he could during her one-week stint at Loew's Capitol.

She was truly in a bad way now. On the day of her opening she was too far gone in brandy to work on top of the grand piano without visibly swaying, and the Capitol's manager said, "Mr. Prince, she will not be allowed to disgrace herself in this theater."

Still classed as a headliner, she was making twenty-five hundred dollars a week while playing next-to-closing spot—and at each performance, an impressive female voice, after a moment of silence, came over the public address system saying only, after a brief intro, "And now, ladies and gentlemen, without further ado, Miss Helen Morgan."

She would come out then from the wings, wearing an off-the-shoulder bouffant floor-length gown that hid her feet as she seemed to drift, head down, walking an obvious chalk line to the microphone at stage center. Once there, holding tight to an old-fashioned, lace-doilied bouquet of tiny roses, she lifted her hand and sang purely, truly, never slurring a note, a full half-dozen songs, which of course included "Bill" and "Can't Help Lovin' That Man," while her eyes glimmered opaquely in a dazzling spot.

She was still lovely to look at, but this season she was far, far out—performing like a docile zombie, with a meek resignation that was almost unbearable to watch.

In the course of her seven days and nights in Atlanta, Donald Prince coaxed her to eat a fair-sized steak, which, to his knowledge, constituted her only intake of solid food. Whatever had lately happened in her private life had been bad, but she was not talking about it. It would seem almost impossible that she was still carrying a torch for Arthur Loew, but then, some women who are monogamous by nature, like the elephant, never forget . . . so who knows? Perhaps this one-man woman was actually still obsessed by "the man who got away."

At the end of her week at the Capitol she moved on, playing the Loew circuit, somehow sustained by brandy, until the end of a tour that brought her back, ill, to Manhattan.

In the fall of 1940 her fans read in Walter Winchell's column that she'd soon be doing a stint at the Famous Door, a small hotspot on West Fifty-second, in the honky-tonk block known as Swing Street.

She was there for several weeks, looking beautiful in her black velvet gowns, but there were times when she must be helped onto the upright piano by waiters who made a stirrup-cup of their hands.

On one occasion, while the crowd overflowed from the club into Swing Street, she sang "Can't Help Lovin' That Man" to perfection. Then, as the cry of "My Bill" . . . sing "Bill" went up, she tried and no words came.

She said, "It's a shame to treat my Bill the way I'm doing tonight." Then, very softly she told her accompanist, "Let's try it again, Professor."

They tried it again, and again no sound issued from her lips. She half whispered then, looking down into all the eager, listening faces, as she touched, in turn, her heart, her brow, and her lips, "I'm so sorry. I have it *here*, but it has to come out *here* and *here*, and I just can't make it.

She slid down from the piano and walked waveringly off toward the back of the club—headed somewhere, anywhere, away from the scene of this sad humiliation. A shocked murmur from the customers rose to shouts of angry disappointment as the small man who managed the Famous Door pushed his way through the crowd, shouting above the clamor, "God damn it, I can't help it if the lady's drunk."

This was the kind of scene that might well have ended another artist's career, but not Helen Morgan's. Somehow she made it through the engagement. There were no ugly references to her pitiable state in the tabloid gossip columns, and somehow, some way, in half a year's time, with guts and determination, this woman rallied her amazing forces for a comeback to life and a measure of stunning success.

On Miami Beach, in 1941, at Jack Dempsey's Pago-Pago Room in the Dempsey-Vanderbilt Hotel, she scored as the outstanding stellar attraction of the winter season. After that she went east again, only to be brought back by popular demand to reopen at the Pago-Pago on July 1 for a three-week run, after which she made surprising news in the Miami *Herald.* "Helen Morgan to Marry," the headline read.

She had met (perhaps in Hollywood) a man named Lloyd Johnson, who obtained a final decree from his wife on July 24 in Miami.

Helen shortly returned from Chicago, where she'd been "summoned by the illness of relatives," and the *Herald* announced that she would march to the altar on Sunday, July 25, "to make it a life partnership with Lloyd Johnson, a Los Angeles auto dealer."

The public "open air ceremonies," beside the swimming

pool at the Dempsey-Vanderbilt cabanas, would be "witnessed by newspaper men, news reel photographers and scores of theatrical friends and associates of the famous star who sang her way into the hearts of millions from the top of a piano."

On Sunday at three o'clock, the couple, both attired in slack suits, were married by Justice of the Peace Ralph Poole, with Bernie Gaines, a former nightclub entertainer, as best man, and a Miss Agnes Delaney as maid of honor. Miss Morgan, in her twenty-fifth year of trouping, gave her age as thirty-six —which, as the retentive reader will observe, would have meant she'd made her debut at seven in that little Montreal bar room.

Helen was, of course, forty-one, and Johnson gave his age as thirty-seven.

For some reason the actual account of the wedding in the Miami *Herald* on Monday was covered in two paragraphs with no pictures, and the paper's amusement page carried an ad that read:

> Jack Dempsey's Pago-Pago room. Tonite: Farewell party to Helen Morgan. No cover.

Helen had told the press that she'd go on with her career, while Johnson would "divide his time between his Los Angeles business and managing the affairs of his bride."

Now, in the last week of July, the couple returned to New York, then moved on to Chicago where Helen was scheduled to star in a vaudeville "tab" abortion of George White's *Scandals*.

In mid-September 1941 Helen arrived in Chicago to open in this condensed *Scandals* revue at the State-Lake Theater. After one night's performance she became suddenly ill and entered Henrotin hospital, where she agreed to submit to an operation by Dr. Samuel J. Taylor to correct a recurrent liver ailment that had plagued her since childhood. (If, as one might have expected, a condition of cirrhosis was involved, the fact was not made public.)

On September 25, after four blood transfusions, her condition seemed greatly improved and Taylor decided to operate the next day.

For a full four days after the operation Morgan seemed to be steadily gaining strength. Then, on the last day of the month, she suffered a serious relapse and, even after further blood transfusions, remained in critical condition.

By October 1 Lulu had come on from the farm, to watch with Lloyd Johnson beside Helen's bed, and to discuss with him, in muted tones, the embarrassing problem of scraping up enough money to pay mounting hospital bills.

Finally, shamefaced, Johnson appealed to the Theater Authority, a "clearing house for all actors' charities." He said he'd paid as much of the bill as he could—thus voicing an apologetic request for which there was no need, since Helen Morgan had contributed, over two decades, thousands of dollars, personally and through a number of benefits, to the support of ill or indigent showfolks.

On October 5 Dr. Taylor told reporters that his famous patient was "very gravely ill," and it must have been on this date that Helen asked for a priest.

She asked to be baptized in the Catholic faith, and her wish was granted shortly before midnight on October 8.

Only her distracted mother and this second husband of just three months—this self-effacing Los Angeles auto dealer— were standing beside the white iron bed where Helen Morgan drew her last, gasping breath.

Next day, when the great black headlines glared above obituaries in the Chicago dailies and the *New York Times* as well as in newspapers published in every major city throughout the United States, a shocked nation rallied to the aid of Lulu and Lloyd.

Manhattan's reporters and columnists might well have had a field day with a wryly ironic situation, but apparently none of them felt a need to revel in outbursts of purple prose, and the *Times* carried only a Chicago Associated Press special bulletin (page 178).

From all over America messages of condolence were received today by her husband, Lloyd Johnson of Los Angeles, and her mother, Mrs. Lulu Morgan of High Falls, N.Y. So [were] offers to help pay for her funeral. For Miss Morgan, whose voice once brought her a sizeable fortune, died penniless in Henrotin Hospital last night.

On October 15, *Variety* revealed that there were three thousand messages and letters, and that the Actors Fund "promptly sent remittances preceding a deluge of offers that came after death. Outside contributions were declined and the funeral expenses were offered by several theater guilds, but her husband said relatives had arranged for interment."

The *Times* item of October 10, which also announced funeral plans, was a model of terse reporting compared to a long, too hasty obituary dashed off the previous day by a Chicago man.

His two-column story related that Tom Morgan was a farmer who'd died when Helen was a child in Danville, that Lulu had once been a schoolteacher, that Helen was "discovered" in 1920 by a Ziegfeld talent scout who put her in *Sally*, and, finally, that she'd reached stardom when, as understudy to Helen Hudson, she'd replaced that ailing lady on the 1925 *Scandals* opening night.

These erroneous statements, destined to be accepted as gospel by theater historians for thirty years, would be of no significance except for one reason already noted in this book: Helen Morgan didn't become a star in the Broadway theater overnight. She made it via the endless drudgery route, singing and acting her way into the hearts of millions for seven years before the autumn of 1932, when her name first appeared in lights above the title of *Show Boat* on the marquee of Philadelphia's Nixon Theater.

For, as every seasoned trouper knows, the overnight stardom cliché is strictly out of old-time movies. This woman made it over a career period of fourteen years, excelling in five show biz mediums: in stage musicals, nightclubs, recordings, network radio, and two outstanding films, *Applause* and *Show Boat*, that proved her to be a first-rate actress.

Morgan (repeat) made it the hard way, all the way up to a kind of stardom that will last as long as her records and those two memorable films can be revived to astonish new generations of fans who were not privileged to see and hear this phenomenon in the flesh.

Inevitably, as "top torcher of the dry era," and the artist for whom the term "torch singer" was coined, she is mentioned by the Prohibition historians along with Texas Guinan as one of two nightclub "queens"—but there the comparison ends.

Guinan was a personality performer who is remembered only in connection with the Prohibition era of which she was a rowdy, rambunctious part. Texas could neither sing nor act, nor did she possess, to even a slight degree, that indefinable quality of which a great star is made.

Her funeral was characterized by the kind of fan hysteria that made a travesty of Rudolph Valentino's passing, but Guinan was never, as was Valentino, a romantic figure idolized by millions. People who knew and liked Texas—reporters, columnists, gangsters, nostalgic nightclub addicts—were sad when she died, but the morbidly curious individuals who broke through police barricades to desecrate her receiving vault and casket were ghouls and nothing more.

If Morgan had died in Manhattan, the demonstration outside some chapel or Catholic church might have equaled the Guinan sendoff, but there would also have been, among the vast uninvited, hundreds of sincere mourners.

Word of her death stunned friends and acquaintances everywhere. And here, in his own words, is the effect this news had on Private First Class George Blackwood, who first heard the news at an obscure Missouri army post in the late afternoon of October 9:

> I was out there at Camp Crowder, a place known to the boys in the service as the most dismal hole in the United States of America, rehearsing *Abe Lincoln in Illinois* which we'd soon be taking on tour under the sponsorship of General Dwight D. Eisenhower.
>
> I was assigned to Special Services—in charge of "Rec"

hall—so I almost never stood retreat. But on this day I was trapped in the evening formation when an announcement of her death came over the P.A. system. My legs buckled beneath me, but of course I couldn't break formation, so I just had to stand there until "taps" were sounded. Then the colonel said "break" and I went over to the Christian chapel to talk with the chaplain, who knew I'd played Steve with Helen in *Show Boat.*

The chaplain did what he could for me. Then I left the chapel, went to my commanding officer, got a pass, and took a bus into Joplin, where I managed, after a long time, to get drunk on three-point beer—the only alcoholic beverage a soldier could get in that little dry, God-forsaken town.

That's how it was with George Blackwood, out there alone in the Missouri boondocks.

On October 10, in the town of La Grange, Illinois, more than six hundred people, including various political notables and a number of famous troupers, turned out to say good-by to a lady and a star who, in her brief lifetime, had become a legend.

At the first service in the small chapel at 110 North La Grange Road, the mourners included Chicago's Mayor Edward J. Kelly, Sophie Tucker (Last of the Red-Hot Mamas), Joe Cook, the nightclub comedian, and the three Andrews sisters.

Two old family friends, Mr. and Mrs. Kenneth Wells, sang a Morgan favorite, "Home Sweet Home," and a Chicago singer whose career Helen had fostered sang "Ave Maria."

After that the cortege moved on to St. Francis Xavier Catholic Church, where Reverend William Hugh O'Brian conducted the requiem mass while Reverend Albert Durant of St. Rita's High School, a friend of Helen's who belonged to a theatrical family, stood in the sanctuary.

In the family group Lulu and Lloyd Johnson sat with two of Helen's aunts—Mrs. Rita McTigue of Dervagrec, Michigan, and Mrs. Elise Dillon of Chicago.

Everything was done with taste, out there in La Grange,

Illinois. Someone (surely the stoic Lulu, aware of what Helen would have wanted) had chosen the pallbearers who would carry her unpretentious casket to the grave in the Holy Sepulcher Cemetery. And someone who must have guessed at the order in which Helen would have liked these pallbearers listed had named them in the Chicago *Times* as John Willis, her "favorite waiter" at Chicago's Chez Paris; Ray Jesselson, a "family friend" from New York; Ed Garney, Jr., a friend in the printing business; a gentleman named Don Chase whose wife was a "friend of Miss Morgan's"; and, last but not least, Jack Irving, secretary to the American Guild of Variety Artists.

Everything had been carried out in good taste, and Helen Morgan, who had felt at home nowhere on Earth except in a place where Lulu was, had gone (perhaps with relief) to her last, peaceful home.

Yes, everything had been in good taste, but, alas, it is not always true that death itself represents a final grief to those who survive a loved one. Sometimes, after the funeral, the press reveals a callous action that stinks of moral corruption and petty greed.

On October 15 Jack Pulaski wrote an accurate, detailed, scornfully truthful two-column obituary for *Variety* in which showpeople were told, in their special lingo:

> Star's first stage job was in George White's *Scandals*, and coincidentally her last appearance before the footlights was in a vaud tab of the same title. She was taken to the hospital in Chicago after playing one day with a condensed revue at the State-Lake but the theater agreed that the unit receive the contract amount in full.
>
> One of the unpleasant reports from Chicago was to the effect that George White could not be located when the need for funds became urgent, that she received but $100 for the day she worked out of $700 which was to have been her salary, despite the fact that White was paid in full and that a sable scarf and silver fox coat were missing from her wardrobe trunk. She had told her husband to sell the furs.

Officials of the American Guild of Variety Artists claim they
sent appeals to White without getting any response.

In another piece, attached to the obit and headed "Proceedings Against White," the story becomes even more appall-
ing:

> Lloyd Johnson, husband of Helen Morgan who died [in
> Chicago] this last week, states that he will prosecute the com-
> plaint entered with the American Guild of Variety Artists
> against George White for failure to pay full salary to the
> singer for a recent engagement at the State-Lake theater here
> with White's *Scandals* unit.
> After appearing for one day in the unit, Miss Morgan was
> rushed to the hospital. Balaban & Katz, in paying off the
> show, paid in full, believing that Miss Morgan was to receive
> full salary. However, White paid the warbler only for one
> day's work, and moved on with the show to Cleveland, where
> she was fully billed. It is reported that White has not yet
> answered any of the calls from Johnson as to salary and the
> return of Miss Morgan's clothes, furs and other belongings.

There it all was in print, this detailed account of White's
shameless actions—but only in *Variety*, the "show biz bible,"
not in the *New York Times* where it could have been read by
thousands of stunned citizens who had loved and cherished
Miss Morgan.

But perhaps it was all right, for Helen, whom Jack Pulaski
had, with admirable understatement, described as "overgen-
erous," was now long past being hurt by any man's meanness.
And, having learned that George White was very small pota-
toes, indeed, compared to Flo Ziegfeld, she might not have
been surprised by his callous actions.

Whether or not she could have forgiven such actions is, of
course, another thing. Sometimes, backstage, when she was
hurt or affronted by someone's deplorable behavior, Helen
Morgan would turn on her heel, speechless, stalk to her dressing room, and stand, fists clenched, swearing at her own white-
faced countenance in a mirror. For some reason (perhaps

because of an overzealous conscience), she could never berate or belittle anyone, no matter how much an abusive person deserved being dressed down.

Helen was not a saint, but she did have saintly qualities— else how could she have moved through the 1920 nightlife netherworld, untouched by surrounding evils?

George Blackwood has always sworn there was an aura about her—something that you could almost see at times. So, if this was true, what was that aura's origin?

Was it some deep, intolerable, secret grief of soul (even more than the sad songs written for her) that probed the hearts not only of squares and gay people, but even of murderous gangsters?

Was she, somehow, to every "ordinary man" sick of the average self-centered female, that always longed for, generous-spirited woman he still hoped to find? And if, when such a man met and talked to her, he encountered a warm-hearted yet oddly reticent woman who seemed in no other way extraordinary, why did this ordinary "Bill," who stayed on to hear her sing once more, still feel that she strangely epitomized that special, as yet undiscovered, ideal lifemate who must exist somewhere?

A careful study of Helen Morgan's psyche reveals a fey creature, elusive as a mythical siren, yet obviously more real, natural, and genuine than most theatrical stars—as real, say, as the "nice little woman next door"—but not, in a clear analysis, innately glamorous as she truly was, very *much* like anyone's nice little neighbor woman.

She was a paradox, right enough, and any nostalgic man could wax lyrical, recalling this "lovely and dreamy" Helen— compassionate, tender, crazily generous, loving, reticent, simple, complex, and always heart-rending perched on those pianos.

In a ridiculous movie made of her life in the 1960s, in which no major event and no character, including her fictionalized self, was authentic, the magical Morgan was depicted as a shabby derelict, stumbling from a skid row bar to collapse in a filthy alley. This was a sin for which a certain

Hollywood producer deservedly suffered at the hands of critics and a public that stayed away in droves.

The whole shabby film was a lie, but it didn't matter. Nobody who loved and remembered Morgan believed one single frame of it, for all the old-timers knew she was never a derelict, nor even a down-and-out alcoholic. She was, rather, a self-abusive, sorrowful, tormented artist, who, depending too much on brandy, nevertheless worked hard, right up to that night in Chicago when she collapsed at the State-Lake theater while laboring under the heartless non-aegis of George White in a "tab" *Scandals* for less than one-fourth her one-time top salary.

She was on the way down just then—but still by no means out, as far as stardom went. Even in that last show she was still beautiful, still her enchanting, enigmatic self . . . and, well . . . since no matter how hard a man tries, he can never finally say just who or what she was—this Circe, Pollyanna, Lady Bountiful, Top Torcher, nightclub charmer—perhaps it is best to leave her now, merely recalling a little poem by Hilaire Belloc entitled *On A Dead Hostess*:

Of this bad world the loveliest and the best
Has smiled and said "Good Night," and gone to rest.

INDEX

Jerome Kern buys rights to
  Show Boat, 32
meets George Blackwood, 106
meets Jerome Kern, 31
researches *Show Boat*, 29–30
sees *James Adams Floating
  Palace*, 30
sends Helen Morgan to drama
  coach, 37
Fetchit, Stepin, 168
Fields, Gracie, 14
Fields, W. C., 36, 83
First Church of Christ Scientist,
  131
Fisher, Harrison, 15
Flippen, Jay C., 103
Follies, 103
Fontanne, Lynn, 105
Ford, Wallace, 30
Francis, Kay, 153
Franklin, Irene, 96, 97
French Trocadero, 9
Frohman, Daniel, 27
Fulton, Donald, 141

Gable, Clark, 140
Gable, William, 140
Garbo, Greta, 161
Garland, Judy, 87
Garland, Robert, 46
Garney, Ed, Jr., 181
Gay Divorce, The, 111
Gershwin, George, 2
Gershwin, Ira, 2
Gibson, Charles Dana, 15
Gish, Lillian, 113
Glad, Gladys, 103, 118
Glorifying the American Girl, 95,
  100
Go into Your Dance, 169
Golden Dawn, 35
Gordon, Gavin, 162
Grand Guignol Repertory, 25
Grant, Cary, 152
Great Gabbo, The, 91
Great Neck, Long Island, 74

Green Mill, 11
Grey, Clifford, 17
Guinan, Texas, 55
  attitude toward Helen Morgan,
    72
  attitude toward prohibition, 69
  business after arrest, 89
  club raided, 63
  debut at Beaux Arts Club, 57
  dies, 162–64
  personality of, 56
  rides in rodeo, 57

"Half-Caste Woman," 103
Hall, Mordaunt, 93, 100
Hammerstein, Arthur, 95
Hammerstein, Oscar, II, 2, 3
  Helen Morgan admires, 38–39
  Helen Morgan's crush on, 98
  Show Boat and, 32
  Sweet Adeline and, 95
Hammerstein, Reginald, 95
Hammond, Percy, 47
Harbach, Otto, 32
Harding, Anne, 95
Harlow, Jean, 87, 152
Harris, Sam, 9
Hecht, Ben, 100
Helen Morgan's 54th Street Club,
  4
  Helen signs contract to appear
    in, 25
Helen Morgan's Summer Home,
  4
  opens, 59
  raided, 63
"Hello My Baby," 96
Henley, Hobart, 100
Hepburn, Katharine, 111
Herbert, Victor, 32
"Here Am I," 96
Herndon, Richard, 23
Hole in the Wall, The, 93
Holiday, 113
Hopkins, Miriam, 93
Hotcha, 119